License to inspire
The Central Illustration Agency

—*Edited by Benjamin Cox*

License to inspire
The Central Illustration Agency

—*Edited by Benjamin Cox*

PIRUM
press

Acknowledgements: This book is the result of a collaboration between CIA, the publishers Pirum Press and designers Staziker Jones. During this process we've been helped enormously by the input of the art directors and editors who have been our creative partners over the years. Ultimately we are only as good as the artists we represent and we're proud to work with such an inspiring stable, but we should also thank the commissioners who've helped bring out the best in them.

No part of this publication may be reproduced, stored in a retrieval system or transmitted, in any form or by any means, electronic, mechanical, photocopying, recording or otherwise, without the prior permission of the copyright owner. Requests for permission should be addressed to the publisher.

The author and publisher have used their best efforts in preparing this book and disclaim liability arising directly and indirectly from the use and application of this book. All reasonable efforts have been made to obtain necessary copyright permissions. Any omissions or errors are unintentional and will, if brought to the attention of the publisher, be corrected in future printings.

A CIP record for this book is available from the British Library

ISBN-10: 0-956572-90-1
ISBN-13: 978-0-9565729-0-5

Designed for Pirum Press by
www.stazikerjones.co.uk

Printed and bound in Italy by Printer Trento Srl. Content, endpapers and cover wrap printed on Munken Print Cream 1.5 115 Gsm. Cover, Cialux cloth on 1.0 mm board. Copy set in Sabon, designed by Jan Tschichold and launched in 1967.

Dedicated...

Contents

In conversation with:

It's about allowing the artist the freedom to interpret the concept, to allow them to do what they do best and contribute in such a way that is truly inspirational…

—I

License to inspire. Now. And how now happened

But first, then.

<u>The 1970s and early 80s were an exciting time to be in the commercial art world. There was an illustration revolution happening, everybody knew each other and the visual trend of the time was slick and technique led. The airbrush was in the ascendency, dominating the advertising world; it was time for a breath of fresh air and London was breathing first.</u>

The illustration scene had been growing in the capital and a small pocket of Covent Garden had become the focus for much of its activity. By 1983 illustration had made its home there, as had Brian Grimwood, a fresh faced and ambitious illustrator.

At that time, Brian was riding the crest of the illustration wave. One of his painted roughs had recently featured on the front cover of *Design* magazine and although the loose, expressive, unfinished execution ran against the grain of his previously published work (and the existing illustrative zeitgeist) it captured the imagination of a commissioning market ready to embrace a new era.

Brian's workload trebled overnight as demand for this new style of work exploded. Unable to leave his drawing board for long he employed a friend, Pam Oskam, to promote his portfolio. Within a fortnight, six or seven artists including Chris Brown, Peter Horridge, Bernard Blatch and Chris McKewan had got in touch to ask if Brian was setting up an agency. The initial response 'of course I'm not' was speedily replaced with 'of course I am' and so CIA was born. Entirely unplanned. The ultimate happy accident.

—Brian's cover for Design *magazine, his preliminary sketch was published in place of the finished illustration.*

—Standing left to right: Chris Brown, Chris McEwan, Sue Curtis, Chloe Cheese. Sitting left to right: Peter Horridge, Brian Grimwood and Pam Oskam.

Though initially small, this new collaboration created a fresh vogue within British illustration for intelligent yet spontaneous, colourful and exciting work and fast became a melting pot of creativity. The select group of artists celebrated their success with a launch exhibition in the spring of '84.

Shirking the obvious, the exhibition was held at the Lighting Workshop, a homeware boutique on Floral Street. This event kick-started a lifelong CIA tradition of throwing up guerilla exhibitions in retail spaces all over central London. Another tradition was firmly established that year when an inaugural artists' Christmas lunch was held at L'Escargot in Soho – cementing our passionate belief that the marketing of illustration should be combined as often as possible with food and drink.

—CIA's first home at Wellington Street,
Covent Garden.

Images: Design and typography by Phil Cleaver. Photography Jennifer Penny.

*—Early CIA promotional material designed by
Phil Cleaver at Et Al*

The reputation of CIA was growing rapidly and Pam Oskam was soon joined by Joanna Marcus. The agency grew in scope as a broad spectrum of new artists came on board and we soon became the recognised port of call for great illustration – whatever the brief.

Our diversity and flexibility in both approach and practice was central to the longevity of the business, allowing it to endure and succeed through the economic thick and thin of the next two decades, and as the roster grew and evolved, so too the team has changed and adapted. The early 90s saw the arrival of Louisa St. Pierre, who brought a renewed sense of vitality to the business, dragging us firmly into the modern technological era. Her innovative, lateral approach to marketing artists enhanced CIA's reputation as a creative agency in its own right and provided a potent legacy when she handed over the running of the agency to Ben Cox and the rest of today's team in 2005.

So, by 2003 the CIA portfolio of artists was an eclectic mix of hugely talented illustrators and the team was looking for new ways to promote and market them. Inspiration came along in the form of Fine & Dandy, one of our creative teams who had created a wonderful piece of authorial promotional work – a whimsically indulgent but beautifully designed almanac. CIA had been toying with the idea of producing a journal of sorts for some time and Fine & Dandy were the catalyst for putting the first issue in motion.

They were appointed as art directors and given a loose brief to contact an inaugural group of artists and pull together what would become the first issue of the *CIA Quarterly*, a 16-page celebration marking the twentieth anniversary of the agency and distributed within the UK's principal commercial art journal, *Creative Review*.

Delighted by the reception the first issue received, the creative gauntlet was thrown down and over a number of years several artists including Simon Spilsbury and Ian Bilbey accepted the challenge, guest editing their own issues of the *Quarterly* as it became known. This name was in fact a celebrated misnomer as the magazine was never actually published quarterly, simply whenever the mood took us. Over the years the format underwent various changes before settling into the newspaper format that was established under the most recent stewardship of illustrators, Dust.

PHENOMENAL SUCCESS.
The Board circulation of
THE CIA
For the Six Days ending
8 P.M. was
3, 102, 936.

THE SHOWING
A DAILY AVERAGE
OF
517, 156
Copies.

The  CIA

Largest Circulation of Any — Agency in the Kingdom

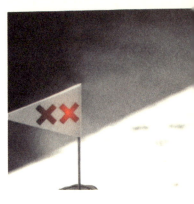

The Central Illustration Agency is extremely proud to present you with the second innovational issue, the eagerly awaited, the beautifully illustrated, the ingeniously designed, the anally directed, the Morse inspected, the ecologically printed, if could go on...) the 'London Issue!'

Our quarterly has been inspired by London old, new, real and surreal. Anything you could imagine—or would rather not—has had some form of consideration while creating this issue. We wanted to celebrate the wonders of this, our home city from temporary ice rinks to the Prospect of Whitby, from Battersea to Sherlock Holmes, from Hyde Park to the Rock & Soul chip shop. It's all there right under our noses and to show this in the best way we know how, we asked the inimitable design collective dust to create this weird and wonderful edition.

CIA have been operating from London since it's birth in 1983 and there is no better way to celebrate the years than to pay a homage to one of the most exciting cities in the world. The Big Smoke has fertilized the growth of our talent and been the rig from which we can offer the creative community some of the most original and critically acclaimed artists.

So far in 2007, we have been very busy bunnies with many high profile UK campaigns and publishing projects coming through our door, to keep you eyes peeled. We have also seen an increase in business, from the Middle East since our birth! Quarterly came out and are spreading ourselves (see design) into the Far East as a taste of Kyoto. A recent visit to Francine La Rosh's Glamourzone is adding to the manic pace we are experiencing. Imagine a Benny Hill sketch show in a tiny Covent Garden office.

We are also very proud to be running the agency in an ecologically friendly way as possible. Let's think about our environment we thought, so our Quarterlies are printed beautifully by The Colourhouse who as well as being an FSC member company, use only soya based inks. Our paper for all of our publications and special projects as well as our stationery is supplied by Paperback and is entirely recycled.

One other thing we need to let you know about is an event we will be holding in the summer. In our opinion, there isn't a better time of year to be in London so if you would like an invite, please do let us know. It will be a big one, showcasing all of our illustrators in a very sexy London location, plenty of fun and a tipple or two as standard. So if you are reading this at the show, say 'ello.

Back Page Illustrations
Front to Back:

Tina Mansuwan
Chris Kasch
Esther Hamaker
Jestte Ford
Jimi Mackay
Ben Wachenje

Centrespread credits

Photograms - C Egginton
Calligraphic lock - R Hertidge
Design and art direction - dust
(www.studio-dust.com)

BLIND MEN IN BLUE

A Licensed House Closed for Three Years and the Police Did Not Know

THE ALLEGED BODY-SNATCHING AT FINCHLEY

NOTHING ELSE FOUND AT WHITEHALL

WARREN TAKES UP THE PEN.

FALSE REPORTS OF AN ARREST

IN THE POLICE COURTS TO-DAY.

The Whitechapel Standard of Comparison.

THE PEOPLE'S POST BOX.

East End Poverty.

ULTRA RADICAL.

WHITECHAPEL — TRAGEDY OR JOKE?

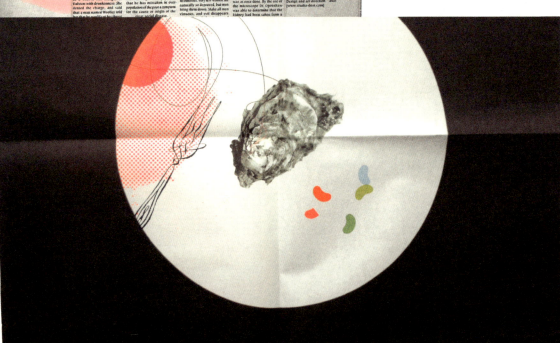

Vierteljährlich Quarterly
zwanzigste twentieth anniversary
jahrestag ausgabe issue
von der from the
zentralen abbildung agentur central illustration agency
CIA

WELCOME to the second issue of CIA Quarterly, the new seasonal publication from the Central Illustration Agency. Every issue is designed by a different artist from our international stable and following the success of Fine and Dandy's stunning launch issue, we are very excited to bring you our February edition, this time designed by Ian Bilbey.

The past few months have seen the arrival in London from New York of the CIA's hugely successful "Celebrity" exhibition, now on it's way to Europe and Japan.

Also Adrian Johnson and McFaul have been at the Coningsby Gallery, Haydn Cornner at the Portal Gallery and Sir Peter Blake has presented the Turner Prize.

FEB 2004

TYPE 2
CIA Quarterly
TYPE 2 CIA
CIA Quarterly
CIA Quarterly
36 WELLINGTON ST COVENT GARDEN LONDON WC2E 7BD.UK.
INFO:@CENTRALILLUSTRATION.COM
WWW.CENTRALILLUSTRATION.COM

Alan Aldridge, Simon Spilsbury, Mick Marston, Brian Grimwood, Mark Thomas and Ian Bilbey have all been busy filling the UK's press and billboards this winter and Kate Miller, Tim Marrs and Gary Taxali among others have been covering some wonderful forthcoming books. We hope you enjoy CIA Quarterly and don't forget to check out the newly relaunched centralillustration.com for a look at all of our artist's folios.

TYPE 2

Edel und Geck

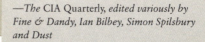

—*The CIA Quarterly, edited variously by Fine & Dandy, Ian Bilbey, Simon Spilsbury and Dust*

CIA
/4 by
year 1
Issue 3

ORTERLY
UGHTILY
RRTILLY
ERLY
T EARLY
ORLEY

I ♥ your work

While the *CIA Quarterly* proved an engaging way to keep clients in tune with the represented artists at a time when web-based marketing was still an emerging opportunity, we continued to look at ways to liberate illustration from its commercial context and provide opportunities for the general populace to experience the work up close. Regular exhibitions were held in many different forms enabling artists to work alongside each other in a variety of platforms. An obvious extension of these events was a festival and the first one, the CIA Summer Festival was held in June of 2004.

Held in the Newburgh Quarter of London's West End, the festival was a show that evolved from a problem that needed solving. Newburgh Street is a hidden treasure: an intimate stretch of cobbles only about twelve shop fronts long which through a quirk of city planning is almost impossible to see unless you're standing on it and as such is often overlooked due to its proximity to its more glamorous neighbour, Carnaby Street.

The street's landlords, Shaftesbury plc were keen to heighten awareness of the Newburgh Quarter, increasing footfall while maintaining the inherent 'cool' of the area. CIA was brought on board to do just that. As Donna Lambert, Head of Communications, puts it, 'I brought CIA on board to facilitate and create an inspiring event concept for the Newburgh Quarter in Carnaby, the purpose of which was to heighten awareness of the area and increase footfall while keeping in line with the cool essence of the street. Their artists teamed up with the retailers of Newburgh to create an on-street gallery for two weeks.'

It was an illustration festival, a street party. Every shop owner and restaurateur in the street got on board with the project and we partnered an illustrator with each one of them, initiating dialogue between artist and business that got to the root of what made each other tick.

—The Tim Marrs imagery for Mooks which prompted the Nike commission

It was an illustration festival; a street party. Every shop owner and restaurateur in the street got on board and an illustrator was partnered with each one, initiating dialogue between artist and business that got to the root of what made each other tick. The illustrators created a bespoke body of work inspired by this discourse which was installed in each space, prominent in the window so that the whole street became an outdoor gallery space with further work displayed inside. The show kicked off on a warm June evening with cold beer, live DJs, animated projections and even a breakdancing crew. Hundreds of people attended that night – many of them had never even known the street existed until then.

Events like this certainly produce a lot of buzz around a group of artists, but commercially do they actually work? A case in point: one of the artists involved in the Newburgh Street project was Tim Marrs who partnered up with Australian fashion label Mooks. As with all the other partnerships on the street, Tim had created a series of artworks for the shop including the windows and one of the people who stopped by was an art director from Nike called Jason Herkert. Over from the US for a holiday, Jason was impressed. 'There was something very refreshing about Tim's work – raw and polished at the same time. His ability to utilise hand-drawn elements combined with self-made type and scans to create a graphic image was truly inspiring.' Back home in New York Jason got in touch and commissioned Tim to produce a series of huge-scale pieces for a major Nike event celebrating the 20th anniversary of the Jordan basketball boot.

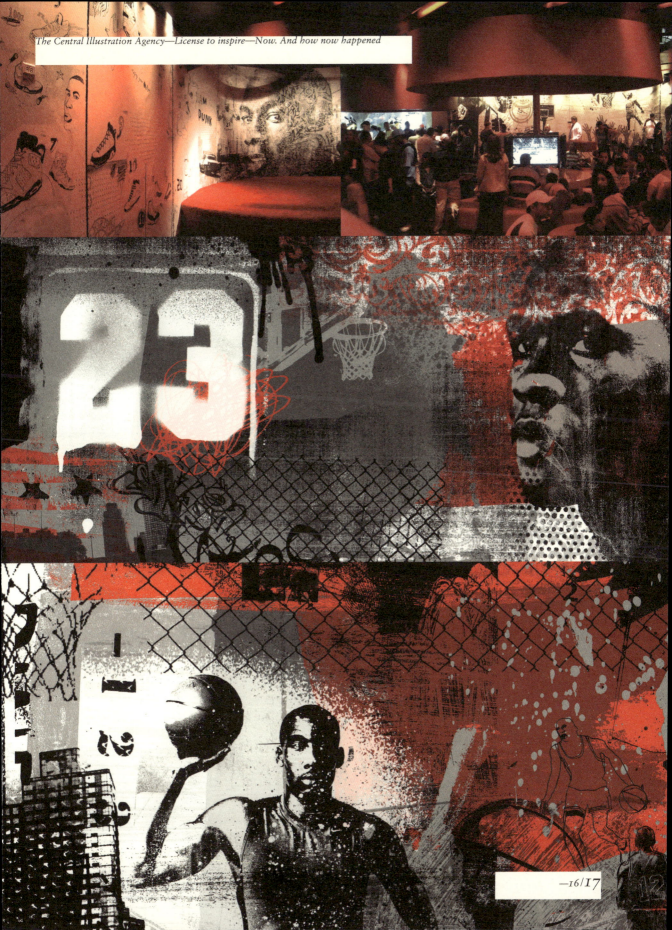

In conversation with <u>Sheri Gee</u>, Art Director
at the Folio Society

'As you probably know, our commissions are mainly for adult fiction – and that's quite rare in the industry, to produce illustrated adult fiction. In general our fiction titles have around 6-12 full page illustrations, usually colour, spaced throughout the narrative, so our illustrators have a wealth of imagery to chose from. To produce amazing work we like to make sure that they have ample time to fully develop their ideas and get under the skin of the brief. It's quite funny for illustrators who are used to editorial schedules of a day or less, to then work with us where they have around 6 months to produce say 8 illustrations.

'Our main thing is attention to detail, making sure the illustrations comply exactly with the book. The more the illustrator has immersed themselves in the book – the characters, the period and place in which it was written – the better. If they start with those strong foundations and adhere to them as the project goes along then they should have enough freedom to express the story using their own visual language, and to create their best work. If an illustrator is constantly having to revise their work because of textual inaccuracies, it can sadly result in their original vision being lost, to the detriment of the illustration. We're a bit of a stickler for detail.

The text itself is the starting point for selecting the right illustrator for the book. Following an initial briefing meeting with Editorial, I read the book and get a good feel for the narrative and the way in which it should be treated. I then have to present my ideas to a small team from Editorial, Marketing & Production before commissioning. Sometimes we'll also have to get approval from the author or the estate, if they're deceased. So often you just see the illustrations or the treatment in your mind as you read the book, and then you have the hard task of trying to find "that" illustrator. Hopefully, once we've found them, everyone agrees!'

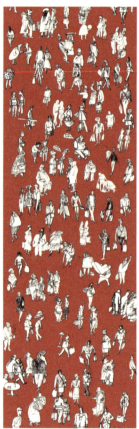

A group of people who attended the Summer Festival had particular reason to be interested in the event. The PR company charged with the remarkable Royal Exchange Building in the City of London were looking to expand its arts calendar and after the success of the Summer Festival we were keen to follow up with a winter one. The Royal Exchange Building was a perfect venue. Originally built in 1565 it stands surrounded by the Bank of England, Mansion House and the Stock Exchange. Today's building was reopened by Queen Victoria in 1884 and it remains one of the most sophisticated places to shop and dine in the City. The stunning interior provided the perfect backdrop for the CIA Winter Festival and the sixteen Corinthian columns that line the former trading floor were hung with 25 feet long banners created by sixteen of our artists.

—Left: Banners from the Winter Festival by left to right, Brian Grimwood, Kai & Sunny, Ray Smith and Simon Spilsbury. Below: Artists gather for the Consequences show.

Photography: Rebecca Lupton

Over the last ten years or so the Internet has brought change to many businesses. It has made the world a very small and accessible place and in the art world physical proximity to the commissioning market has become less important, allowing artists to carve out a successful career without needing to be based in the capital. However as increasing numbers of CIA artists have moved away and the ranks of internationally based artists increased, the need to maintain our sense of creative community has become all the more crucial. The Consequences show held in 2007 faced this challenge by bringing CIA's illustrators together to create a single, collaborative artwork.

An empty retail unit in Covent Garden was commandeered and the artists were briefed on the project. Each one would be given an A2 panel and all of these panels would join up to create a single landscape artwork, the height of the panel, but 90 feet long. Each artist was provided with a digital template of their panel, blank except for a key line representing an undulating horizon. When joined together, this horizon line of hills and valleys would extend seamlessly throughout the entire length of the artwork. They could fill their landscape with whatever they wanted, but they were instructed to communicate with their neighbours, informing each other how their works were developing and creating visual connections between their pieces.

—*Panels from the 90 foot long Consequences landscape. Left to right, Spiral Studio, Darren Hopes, Benjamin Wachenje, Dust, Chris Kasch and Ray Smith*

In this way the artists were forced to educate themselves about the methodology of their neighbours and then question how that method could connect with their own. The running order was composed specifically to ensure that the artists encountered other artists using media very different from their own and in many cases paint would run across into a digital piece and vice versa.

One of the fundamental differences between authorial and commercial practice is that the latter requires the expression of someone else's concept within a framework that may well have been delicately constructed for entirely valid (if creatively frustrating) commercial reasons. However some of the best work can be born of the conflict inherent in the process and the Consequences show proved exactly that. It is easy to position the commissioning client as the creative enemy, the imposer of boundaries, the builder of the brick walls that illustrators can be found beating their heads against but the degree of interaction and questioning forced by the show illustrated that this conflict plays a valuable role in the informed organic development of an artist's work.

We find the third person that is produced when a creative commissions another creative can often be greater than the two constituent parts. The results are more rewarding than either could have created without the resolution of the conflicts generated by the commercial remit of the job, and certainly not without each other's individual talents. Hand in hand with us as agents, the commissioning team needs to strike a balance during this artistic partnership, knowing how to allow the mutual inspiration to flow between art director and illustrator, while keeping a solid grasp on the logistics of the project and the ultimate objectives of the brief.

Changing times have broadened our approach to the marketing of illustration and, like anyone involved in communication today, a technological depth has developed within our language. The roots of the agency are still firmly embedded in the traditions of getting out there and meeting people but it's no longer enough to hold printed portfolios and publish a website – the world has become far too hungry for fresh stimulus. Social media has become a tremendously fertile arena with the immediacy of tweeting and blogging playing a pivotal role in the dialogue with the outside world.

James Davidson of weheart.co.uk has seen a massive shift in the prevalence of blogs and social media in the marketing of illustration. 'Our online creative lifestyle guide has a homepage dedicated to a selected daily feed of all the simply brilliant designers, illustrators and photographers who send their work in. Illustrators have definitely become really switched on to this arena and the freedom to put their unique stamp on the work they produce without getting bogged down in fashion and trends. Our readership is more than aware that fashions come and go. Jaw-droppingly original ideas have lasting impact.'

Of course, dialogue flows in all directions and CIA has grown and developed in response to direct feedback from its clients. Increasing demand for typographic treatments to complement the artwork we were producing developed into a new department within the agency which Jules, our senior agent at CIA, set up a few years ago. We proudly represent several artists for whom illustrative letterform is a linchpin of their visual language, Peter Horridge, Sarah J. Coleman, John Spencer to name three, but many more including Kai & Sunny, Tim Marrs and Harriet Russell regularly employ hand rendered type within an otherwise richly pictorial style.

Hand in hand with us as agents, the commissioning team needs to strike a balance during this artistic partnership, knowing how to allow the mutual inspiration to flow between art director and illustrator, while keeping a solid grasp on the logistics of the project and the ultimate objectives of the brief.

—*Typographic illustrations by Peter Horridge (above),*
Jitesh Patel (right) and Nik Ainley (below)

—Kai & Sunny (top), Sarah J Coleman (above)
and Jonas Bergstrand (left)

Jubileumsfest för Astrid Lindgrens Barnsjukhus 10 år. Fira Pippidagen 2008!
Skansen, torsdagen den 12 juni från 13.00. Artistgala 18.30. www.astrid-barn.nu

FOUND ART - 'SCRAP BOOK SAILOR'

CHANGE HAPPENED.

The latest branch to the CIA tree is its shop – something we really should have done years ago. For a long time clients and the public alike had been coming to our shows or visiting our website and asking if the work was for sale. We never had an organised way of answering that question until we bit the bullet in the summer of 2008 and started putting together our online shop to sell prints and products from our gang of illustrators. Months of research into the wonderful world of retail by our PR guru Alicja, turned her into a *bona fide* shopkeeper and culminated in our new baby launching with a physical exhibition that October.

Particularly exciting was that a great many of our illustrators were putting their work into a sales environment for the first time, but we wanted the opportunity of owning these pieces to be accessible to all so resisted the temptation to charge exclusive prices for what was very exclusive work. The packed launch show saw many editions sell out and the business has continued to grow online at an alarming rate with the range extending from art prints to totes, toys, tattoos and the ever popular CIA Calendars.

One of the annual collaborative projects which has become an essential part of the agency's output is the CIA Calendar. This was a tradition some years ago when it was a page-a-month affair but Jules took up the running and reworked it into the collectable it is today. A new theme each time and now boasting a page per week allowing us to showcase the majority of our bunch every year, it's in the CIA Shop but also stocked in an increasing number of stores in the UK and abroad including Magma, SCP and the Design Museum. We hear that buyers are making paper sculptures from the pages as the weeks go by. An exhibition in the making perhaps...

In conversation with <u>Sir John Hegarty</u>, BBH

'When it comes to creativity, there is a very interesting journey in going from good to great. They say that "good" is the enemy of "great" and how you get from one to the other is a fascinating process that really does consume me.

Everybody will work in different ways and that is why inspiration is so key. We need to be constantly challenged, constantly driven forward and we never know where it's going to come from, it's a wonderfully complex area. In terms of the collaborative relationship between art director and illustrator, we must expect an art director to do just that; direct. They should provide the idea, know the visual tone and control the project, but also be prepared to be challenged and allow for serendipity. Illustrators are ideas people too and it's always interesting to have that conversation with them and share the process. The crucial thing is to respect your suppliers.

CIA and BBH emerged at the same time in the early 80s. Huge skill and understanding is gained from experience, but we also have to understand that we are in an industry akin to fashion, it's about what's next, not what's been. You can't come in and have an idea you had yesterday, it can't even be like yesterday's idea, it has to be completely new and there is an inherent feeling in the industry that younger people will deliver that. The bizarre conundrum of it all is that you have to have maturity to understand the creative process. I think the great skill is to mature immaturely.'

Seasons shift within illustration as fluidly as in any other creative discipline. A strong visual movement will naturally provoke an equally strong counter movement and the slick, lavish Photoshop revolution of yesterday has led to today's rebirth of craft. It can be said that the homemade quality of print-made, painted or constructed imagery feels emotionally appropriate to a period of financial hardship as it is more comforting and human. What effect a period of growth will have on this trend remains to be seen.

But one result of this revival in handmade illustration has been the opportunity to experience at first hand the creative process at work, where illustration becomes installation and the execution of a large scale commission becomes performance. So we won't hazard to predict what the next aesthetic boom may be. However, the increasing liberation of commercial art from the 2-dimensional confines of the printed page or billboard site is increasingly endorsed by visionary retail clients, venue owners and architectural firms inviting artists to engage with their space in an altogether more spectacular and theatrical fashion.

A 3-dimensional graphic approach to retail window display is par for the course, but the team at Liberty, led at the time by Katie Baron and Faye McLeod, broke new ground several years ago by inviting Andrew Foster, illustrator and head of course at Central Saint Martins, to comprehensively unleash his particularly physical brand of image making onto the outside of the entire store's windows. Armed with mops, rollers, litres of paint and reams of pre-printed paper, he threw, ripped and pasted together the most controversial Liberty windows to date, a process that lasted a week as he progressed around the store capturing the attentions of a mystified public as well as the Metropolitan Police.

A fantastically energetic piece of highly contemporary display art, thickly layered and exposed to the ravages of wind, rain and prying hands engaged the public as never before, prompting complaints from the store's more dusty patrons but fanfaring a new 'think big' approach to collaboration with illustrators and inspiring the creators of London Fashion Week and Kiehls to work with Foster on future projects.

Since then this hands-on approach to space-invasion has flourished. Why digitise and print an artwork when an artist or team

—Jeff Nishinaka's paper sculpture for the Ana Hotel and the Pop Up Pirates bar

of artists can walk into a bar, flagship store or ad agency, absorb the sense of structure, scale and light and respond in an entirely unique manner, creating a period of performance art which fires the imagination of all who witness it and leaves behind a piece of work that's sensitive to the space on a fundamental level. Kai *&* Sunny have fitted out hotel rooms with bespoke wall coverings and furniture, Jeff Nishinaka has grown paper trees for Bloomingdales and Paul Wearing has created building-sized window art for O*&*M in Chicago.

Today, Pirates are collaborating with bar and restaurant owners Mothership Group, moving into their venues in Clerkenwell and Shoreditch creating 3-dimensional sculptural elements to accompany the wall pieces that are transforming the spaces into reworked temporary pop-up bars within bars. As Jon Ross of Mothership says, 'We are more than aware that over the years our venues have become surrounded by new bars that appeal to a very similar demographic. We need to get creative and generate increasingly stimulating environments to engage our client base. As a team, Pirates have the strength in numbers to be able to assess a space, take on board the architectural quirks and historic relevance of a building and treat it with a completely individual approach.'

As I write, one of our illustrator/art directors Alex Turvey is partnering with Levi's as part of their new exhibition at the Regent Street store. Inspired by circus mirrors and currently standing in the front windows his three giant mirror sculptures bring the passerby into the picture as the distorted reflection of their own image becomes the artwork. Illustration in its more conventional application can be a tremendously powerful and emotive form of visual communication, but there is something unavoidably arresting about introducing that third dimension, pulling it shouting from a wall, ceiling or floor, that looks set to be an increasingly dominant feature of our commercial practice for some time yet...

—Alex Turvey working on the Levi's installation.
Photographs by Tom Bunning

An integral part of the CIA philosophy is that everyone within the agency comes from a creative background. Each member of the 2010 team is an image maker in their own right which creates a greater level of empathy with our artists and the clients that commission them. It has evolved into the tight group of twenty-to-thirty-something-year-old art school graduates it is today. After studying photography, Ben Cox has been representing artists since 1999 and joined CIA in 2003, running things since 2005 and keeping a weather eye on the bigger, strategic picture. This is, of course, made achievable by having a crew who have developed their own specialist roles in the agency and look after the detail.

Jules Beazley joined CIA shortly after Ben in 2003 having just graduated in Graphic Design. Our lead agent she's never happier than when she's at the negotiating table, putting the right creatives together in the right way. Alicja McCarthy came on board in 2005, bringing with her a degree in Advertising and a keen talent for spreading the CIA word into areas hitherto untapped. She runs the shop and heads up our PR and events.

Rhiannon Payne has been a CIA agent since 2007 moving straight into the industry from an Illustration degree and tasked specifically with hitting the creative industries around the UK when she's not at London HQ. Sarah Johnson keeps the ledgers balanced but even the brains behind the book-keeping is our go-to resource for cultural bulletins.

The life of the freelance commercial artist can be a daunting and isolating experience, especially for those who have only recently entered the fray and are adjusting to life without a support group of like-minded people. The artists range in age from early twenties to early seventies and are far flung as New York, Bangkok and Melbourne. Of course the principle responsibility is to market and protect their work, but alongside this we aim to provide a sense of creative community, bringing the group together to work on collaborative projects that we commission in-house.

The artist and the client remains entirely central to CIA's ethos and creating new and innovative ways to marry the two underpins the future of the business. The objective has always been and will continue to be, to create as many platforms as possible for clients to encounter the work produced by the artists and while online activity, presentations and exhibitions form a crucial part of the marketing strategy, access to clients remains key. In conversation with Julian Cave of BBH, we discussed the importance of bringing the work of our artists into an agency's studios to fire the imaginations of his creative teams in as direct a way as possible.

As Julian put it, CIA seeks a *'license to inspire'*.

An integral part of the CIA philosophy is that everyone within the agency comes from a creative background. Each member of the 2010 team is an image maker in their own right which creates a greater level of empathy with our artists and the clients that commission them.

2

The mechanics of a job: a relatively simple case study

Book cover illustration by Kai & Sunny
1001 Dreams by Jack Altman
Commissioned by Jantje Doughty for
Duncan Baird Publishers

Amongst a tremendously varied portfolio of work including global ad campaigns, packaging and installation projects, Kai & Sunny have arguably been involved in some of the most iconic book jacket work of the last ten years.

At the beginning of 2010, the design team at Duncan Baird Publishers were researching creative routes for a forthcoming title dealing with the interpretation of dreams. Their research took them to the CIA website and certain ethereal, almost hypnotic visual qualities inherent in aspects of Kai & Sunny's folio struck a chord with where DBP wanted to go.

Editor Jantje Doughty contacted the agency with the bare bones of the proposed creative brief. Briefs differ greatly from project to project, company to company. Often, especially in the advertising arena, those briefs can be really very prescriptive, the concept resolved through rounds of research and internal discussion before it reaches the studio of the chosen artist.

In this case, the publishers wanted something evocative of the surrealism of a dream state and referenced Escher as a visual conversation starter but the brief was relatively open, allowing Kai & Sunny to get a handle on the text and to inspire the work. A lovely way to start and in principal the boys were keen to take the project on, especially as this was the first book in a potential series.

Rhiannon, the CIA agent who took the enquiry, needed to establish some fundamental parameters, common and essential to any commissioned project. The first thing to establish was the schedule; we needed a deadline for the delivery of work in progress and an ultimate date for the delivery of final art. In this case the client had two weeks for Kai & Sunny to get the initial round of development work to them and a further month for creation of final art. This suited the boys' diary.

  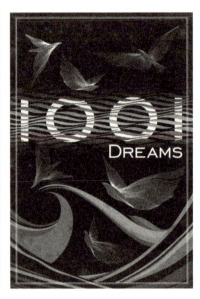

Theoretically, a first draft will be submitted, feedback from the client taken on board and any necessary adjustments made. Having had those adjustments approved by the client, the artist will proceed to final art. Approval of final art should be a happy formality, creases having been ironed out in the earlier stages. In reality minor tweaks may be needed to absolutely nail the final art and this is usually acceptable – all part of the fluidity of the creative process. It is one of CIA's responsibilities to ensure that the process is allowed to flow but that the number of amendments remains within reasonable bounds and true to the original brief.

Second, Rhiannon needed to establish the fee and any contractual/rights details. CIA needed to satisfy itself that Duncan Baird would be licensed to use the artwork in specific media directly related to the book in question, that all other rights would remain the property of the artist and that the fairly negotiated fee covered the required usage license plus the sheer creative talent that our boys would bring to the table.

A fee was discussed and accepted for the cover art and the license details talked through and confirmed in a Purchase Order or Confirmation of Assignment – an utterly crucial document that states in no uncertain terms that a very specific deal has been struck and that at the appropriate time our invoice for work done will be honoured.

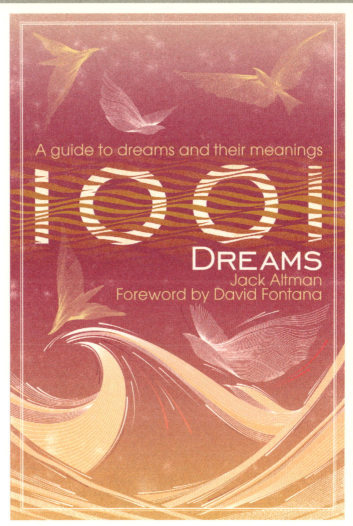

A guide to dreams and their meanings

1001

DREAMS
Jack Altman
Foreword by David Fontana

Having set the ground rules, the creative process could start in earnest. Rhiannon introduced Jantje to Kai & Sunny and then stepped back to an observational position, allowing them to liaise directly throughout the visual process.

Kai & Sunny visited the publishers for a face to face meeting with Jantje Doughty and Art Director Roger Walton. It was a great session as it was very discussion led rather than instructional and prescriptive.

Initial work was delivered in monotone, focusing attention on ambience, weight and form. As the job progressed feedback from the client included requests to further develop and enhance the waves towards the bottom of the image and discussions as to where supporting cover text could sit.

The regular and open communication between commissioner and artist resulted in a cover that all parties were extremely happy with. The job was invoiced and the collective team went on to start on the second in the series of books.

In conversation with <u>Paul Slater</u> and <u>Tom Conran</u> at the Cow

'There's an irreverent anarchistic streak that runs through the British character, Paul Slater's work taps into this and then goes for a ramble. The paintings I have managed to collect over the years bring me endless joy. The first painting I bought was commissioned when we first opened the Cow in the 90s, the picture covers a complete wall, you can't help but run into it. The painting depicts a rural scene complete with pastors, lords, hunters and farm workers, but the hunters are prawns and the farm workers are crabs, the horses are fish and everything is under the sea. I have seen folk sit at the bar clutching their pint completely transfixed by the picture, I think this is part of the attraction, the double take or the questioning of something that seems perfectly normal on one level but forces us to think harder on another'. — *Tom Conran*

'I have an acute visual memory for things. I noticed I was under this spell, drawing from life all the time and at the end I had books and books of really shitty half-done drawings. And then one day back in the 70s, I was on a bus going past Hyde Park looking out the window and there's this bloke walking down the street. It was the funniest figure I'd ever seen. He had a hitch-hikers back pack on, one of those really big ones with the bars on it and he had this long straight curtain of hair, a baseball cap, and the tightest pair of shorts I'd ever seen in my life. And he was bent double, walking along, and there were leaves bustling round him, but the best thing was, there was this fucking bird just hovering above his head. In that split second I saw him, it looked like it was the Holy Ghost following him.

I got back to the studio and I sat down and I drew it from memory and I thought, that's better than if I'd taken a photo. I saw everything I needed to see, no extraneous details that didn't matter, I just saw the essence of the thing, and I thought I've been denying my visual memory. I draw better from memory than I do sitting in front of the thing.

And there's a coda to that story. Years later, twenty years later, I was up in the Lake District driving along in the car on this foggy day and I saw this figure, bent double with a pack on his back, no hair now, and I swear to God, the fucking bird was there. It was the same guy! And I thought, I wonder if he knows the bird's there, he hears this fluttering in his ears the whole time, it sits on his bedhead when he goes to bed and when he looks in the mirror to shave it just ducks behind him...'. — *Paul Slater*

'Unbound to any specific
is free to express their p
with a limitless variety of
developing a language a
as their fingerprint. The
be celebrated and so CIA
occupy a stylistic niche ir
always sought to repres
very best commercial a
they're saying, however t

medium, an illustrator

ception of the world

visual approaches,

unique to themselves

esulting diversity is to

have never sought to

he agency market, but

t a broad range of the

ists, resolved in what

y may be saying it.'

3

The artists

12foot6/The 3D Agency/Ahoy There/Nik Ainley /Tatiana Arocha/Artbombers/Tom Bagshaw /Andrew Bannecker/Jonas Bergstrand/Ian Bilbey /Sir Peter Blake/Bernard Blatch/Greg Bridges /Christopher Brown/Mick Brownfield/Lesley Buckingham/Susan Burghart/Nishant Choksi /Stanley Chow/Sarah J. Coleman/Haydn Cornner /Jimi Crayon/Dust/Tristan Eaton/Max Ellis/Fine & Dandy/Jeff Fisher/Jessie Ford/Andrew Foster /Nathan Fox/Jonathan Gibbs/Chris Gilvan Cartwright/Good Wives & Warriors/Brian Grimwood/Martin Haake/Pete Harrison /Lee Hasler/Sara Hayward/David Holmes/Darren Hopes/Peter Horridge/David Hughes/M. H. Jeeves/Kai & Sunny/Chris Kasch/Carol Lawson /Tina Mansuwan/Tim Marrs/Mick Marston /MEGAMUNDEN/Chris McEwan/Clare Melinsky /Kate Miller/Dave Needham/Gary Neill/Jeff Nishinaka/Paul Oakley/Nigel Owen/Jackie Parsons/Jitesh Patel/Pirates/Wendy Plovmand /Ulla Puggaard/Maria Raymondsdotter/John Royle/Harriet Russell/Jeremy Sancha/Yuko Shimizu /Paul Slater/Ray Smith/John Spencer/Simon Spilsbury/Spiral Studio/Louisa St. Pierre/Mark Thomas/Alex Turvey/Benjamin Wachenje/Paul Wearing/Richard Wilkinson/Mike Wilks

—12foot6

12foot6 are moving artists, character builders, animators. They create beautiful illustrations and make them move. BAFTA-nominated for The Sensibles *(Jetix)*, they make adverts for various companies like Virgin Media and are the creators and broadcasters of Dog Judo.

—The 3D Agency

This team of artists have been working for over 16 years producing the highest quality 3D work for print and animation. Catering worldwide for the advertising and entertainment industries they have a range of technical and creative specialists within the agency who can work with any brief, big or small.

—Ahoy There

Ross Crawford and David Souch make up this award-winning creative partnership who comfortably straddle the visual disciplines of illustration, graphic design and typography, a diversity that has brought their talent to bear on numerous branding, fashion and advertising projects at home and abroad.

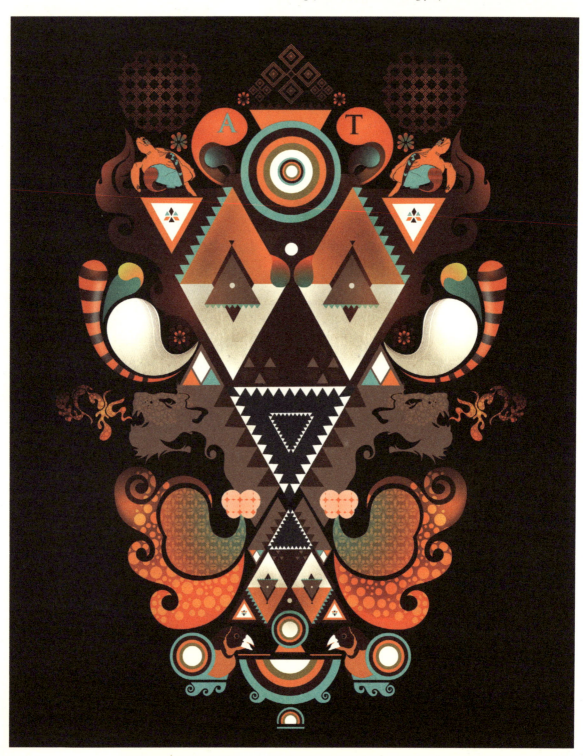

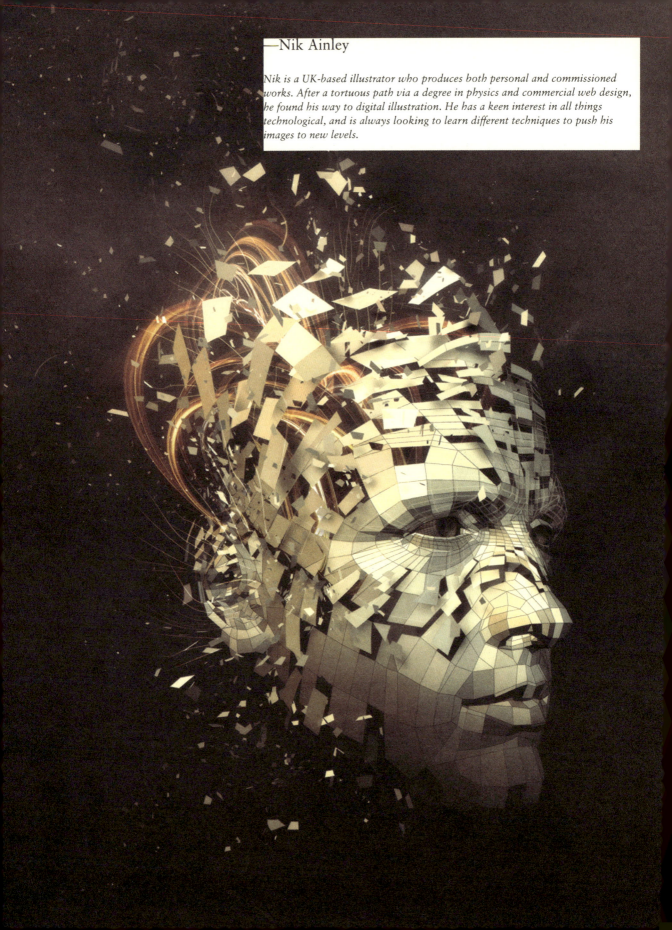

—Nik Ainley

Nik is a UK-based illustrator who produces both personal and commissioned works. After a tortuous path via a degree in physics and commercial web design, he found his way to digital illustration. He has a keen interest in all things technological, and is always looking to learn different techniques to push his images to new levels.

—Tatiana Arocha

*Born and raised in Columbia, Tatiana moved to New York City in 2000 and
has worked there as an art director, designer and animator giving her a broad
understanding of the industry as a whole. Collaboration is king for Tatiana
and she still works in direction and animation as well as illustration.*

—Artbombers

Artbombers are a UK illustration duo who love mixing the elegance of traditional line with the smooth renderings of digital, perfecting a raw and pure symbiosis from the collision of the two disciplines.

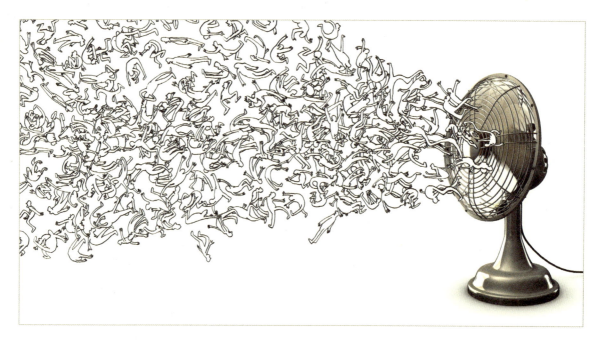

—Tom Bagshaw

Based in Bath, Tom's work leans towards figurative fine art genres and his soft painterly images are, in fact, created digitally. Combining fantastical elements with fashion model hybrids his work is weirdly wonderful, and as well as working extensively in advertising and publishing, his art prints are quite stunning.

—Andrew Bannecker

Andrew began a career in advertising before his desire to create original artwork led him to a life of illustration. Surrounded in his studio by random collected ephemera, he creates richly narrative work that captures the imagination. Andrew lives and works in Washington DC.

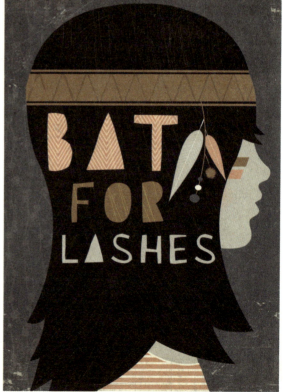

—Jonas Bergstrand

Jonas was born in Stockholm 17 minutes after his twin brother Magnus. The creative black sheep in an otherwise medical family, Jonas takes a diagnostic approach to design and illustration. He thinks behind the surface, the problem solving aspects governing much of the beauty of his work.

—Ian Bilbey

London-born Ian Bilbey studied graphic design at the RCA. His work remains influenced by his design background with a prominent concentration on colour and line, but laced with a quirky Britishness. He now lives in the English countryside and in his spare time races vintage sports cars.

—Sir Peter Blake

Peter graduated from the RCA in 1956 having also completed his National Service. He received the Leverhulme Research Award to study popular art whilst travelling Europe and went on to teach for several years at various London Art Schools, all the while working and exhibiting. His first solo show was held in the Portal Gallery in 1962 and since the early 70s his work has regularly been exhibited in one-man shows and retrospectives around the world. In 1981 he was elected a member of the Royal Academy and in 1994 was made the Third Associate Artist of the National Gallery. He was knighted in 2002.

—Bernard Blatch

Bernard began studying at Wimbledon School of Art the year World War II ended. He worked for the BBC and Thames Television graphics departments before becoming an illustrator. He defected to Norway in 1977 to continue illustrating and teaching at Oslo College of Art & Design. In '93 he was elected into the Alliance Graphique Internationale and in 2002 was awarded the first Classic Award issued by Grafill.

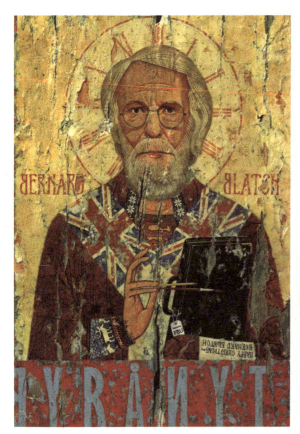

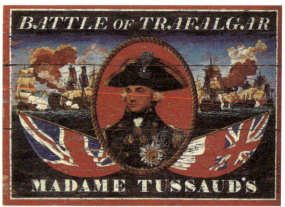

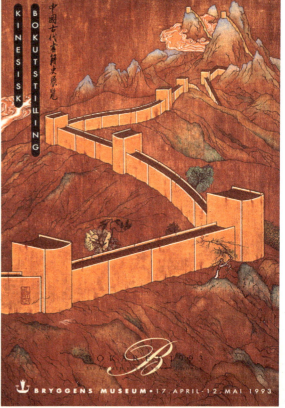

CELEBRITY

—Greg Bridges

Greg is based in Sydney, Australia, and his early professional years were spent as a designer and art director, granting him a keen understanding of the industries that now commission him. Inspired at an early age by cinema and surrealism, his enigmatic, futuristic work is inspired not only by the spectacular surroundings of his local area but also from extensive world travel.

—Christopher Brown

After studying at the RCA Christopher assisted Edward Bawden who encouraged him to explore linocutting. During his career Christopher has exhibited at The Royal Academy and the Victoria & Albert Museum and worked extensively in the publishing industry. He lectures at Liverpool School of Art (John Moores University) and at Central Saint Martins in Fashion Design Menswear.

PRONTO DA CUCINARE!

—Mick Brownfield

*Perhaps unsurprisingly, Mick is a passionate movie-goer and comic collector.
He was born in London and has worked there ever since in pretty much every
area of Design, Advertising, Editorial and Publishing for clients as diverse as
Disney, Coca-Cola and Shell.*

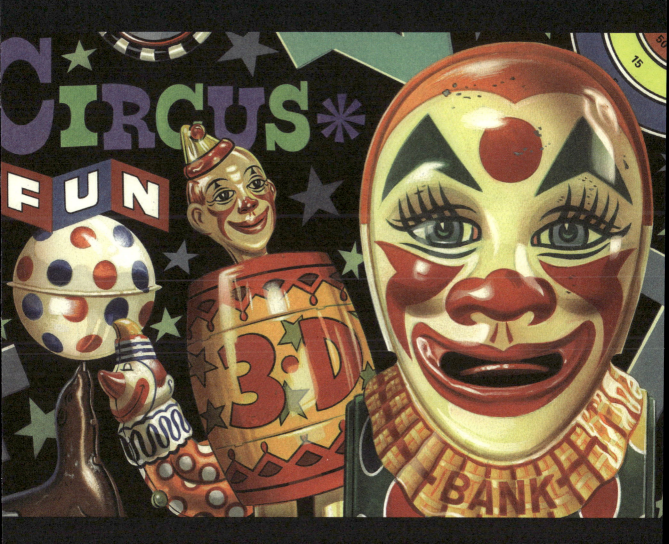

—Lesley Buckingham

Lesley lives in the fertile glades of the English countryside where the enchanting surroundings of her garden studio permeate her illustration work, textiles and model making. Illustrating for packaging and books – whether her own or someone else's – Lesley also regularly exhibits around the UK.

—Susan Burghart

Susan worked as a graphic designer for eight years before attending Camberwell College of Arts in London in 2006 to re-train as an illustrator and her work features in the permanent collection of the University of the Arts London. Susan enjoys working digitally as well as experimenting with distressed effects through collage and screen printing. She aims to achieve something fresh and edgy but with a touch of elegant nostalgia.

—Nishant Choksi

The wit and charm of Nishant's award-winning work, especially his character illustration, has kept him extremely busy at home and abroad working with a diverse range of clients from the Guardian *to* Vanity Fair, Vodafone *to* Dyson. *He lives and works in Brighton.*

—Stanley Chow

It's all about Manchester for Stan. Born there, raised there, studied there, lives and works there. A club DJ, he started designing and illustrating flyers and posters for the venues he played and it all kicked off from there. Stanley has worked prolifically throughout the Design, Editorial and Advertising sectors and is a favorite regular visitor to CIA Towers.

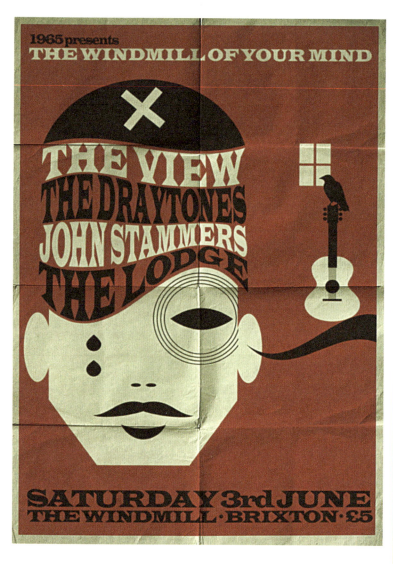

—Sarah J. Coleman

Sarah's route to illustration and typography has been semi-conventional. On the one hand she did an art degree, on the other hand she dipped into pirate radio, theatre, prop-making and typesetting obituaries. Now she's in her second decade of wrapping her perma-stained fingers around words and pictures for advertising, identities, packaging and book covers.

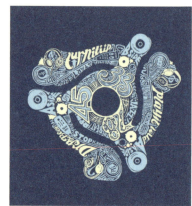
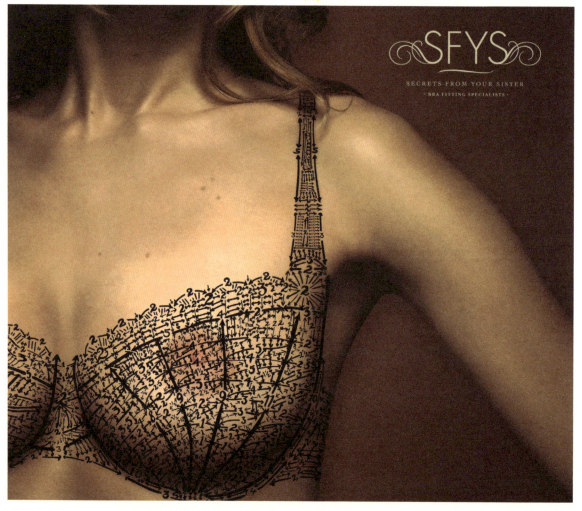

is for Horror,
poisonous ground.

is for atmosphere,
polluted, unsound.

is for Levels,
too high, make you sick.

is for Lifestyle,
a concept, a trick.

O is for on,
all the time.
Standby!

W's waste,
filling ground,
piling high.

An 'E for emissions,
nought out of ten.

Another for energy,
well run out —
what then?

is for new,
do you need it?
Do you?

—Haydn Cornner

Born in a room above his grandmother's haberdashery shop, Haydn, a sailor's son, led a peripatetic childhood and travel has been a constant source of inspiration ever since. Following a stint performing with a touring comedy show, he began concentrating on painting in the early 80s. Haydn has illustrated numerous books and has regular one man shows here in Mayfair.

—Jimi Crayon

What hasn't Jimi done? He's exhibited alongside Gormley and Rankin, customised shoes for Thierry Henry and sold his work to Immodesty Blaze. An irrepressibly positive outlook brings an enthusiastic and vibrant edge to his imagery. He'll probably be in space this time next year.

—Dust

Established in 2000 and based in the industrial city of Sheffield, Dust is a commercial graphic arts and design studio run by Patrick, Alun and Pamela, all of whom met 15 years ago studying at Leeds Metropolitan. They love what they do; its heritage, its inceptions and its outcomes.

Fly fishing may be a very pleasant amusement; ⓡ but angling or float fishing I can only compare to a stick, and a string, with a worm at one end and a fool at the other.

Samuel Johnson attributed, in *Hawker Instructions to Young Sportsmen* 1859

Also attributed to Jonathan Swift in *The Indicator* 27 October 1819

—Tristan Eaton

Born in Los Angeles in 1978 and now based in Brooklyn, Tristan's a graffiti artist turned illustrator turned toy designer. His early days were spent painting anything from billboards to dumpsters wherever he went. He designed his first toy for Fisher Price aged 18 and has since become a driving force in the world of 'Designer Toys' as well as illustrating for creative agencies all over the world. His work is held at the Cooper Hewitt Museum as well as MOMA.

—Max Ellis

Our resident creative chameleon, Max trained as a precision engineer before taking a degree in Illustration and Photography. Paint was his thing and he can still produce magic with pen and pencil, but after ten years of craft he went digital. Currently straddling all forms of creative media including video and photography, Max is the ultimate visual problem solver.

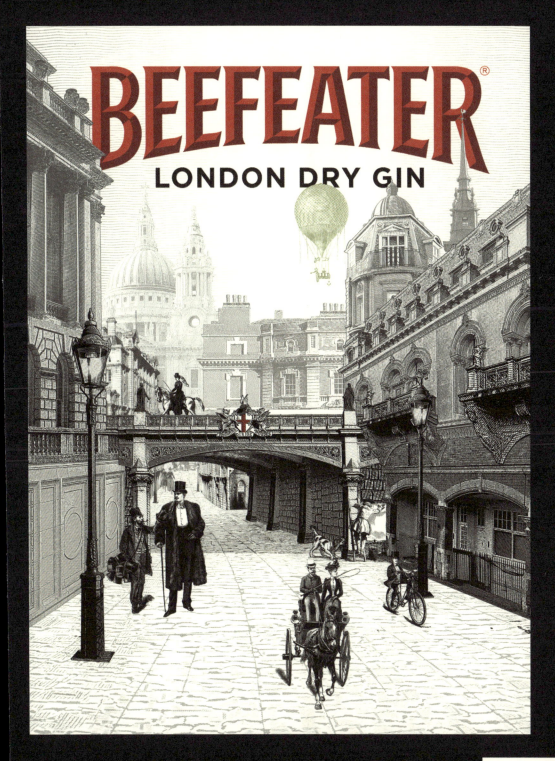

An illustration collaborative forged in 2001 between the team at Dust and Mick Marston, Fine & Dandy have produced illustration for brands, advertising and exhibition as well as designing exceptionally inspiring almanacs and quarterly journals for the enlightenment of the creative community worldwide.

fig. i

fig. ii

fig. iii

fig. iv

Pictured
**Fine & Dandy —
Miscellanea
Botanical**

fig. i Branta leucopsis
fig. ii Borometz
fig. iii Mandrake
fig. iv Raskovnik

—Jeff Fisher

Jeff hails from Melbourne Australia where he studied Fine Art Film and Animation at Preston Institute of Technology in the 70s. He flirted with London for a while before settling down in France in 1993. The bulk of Jeff's work has been book cover design as well as working in design and exhibiting regularly in Paris and London.

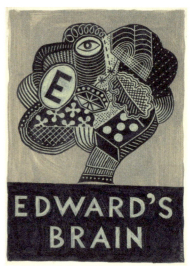

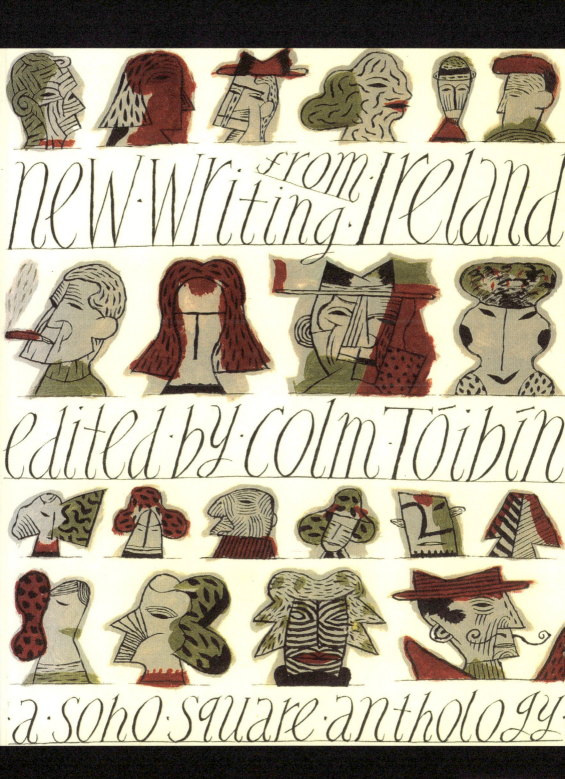

new·writing·from·Ireland

edited·by·colm·Tóibín

a·soho·square·anthology

—Jessie Ford

Jessie lives and works in sunny Brighton. Her approach combines graphic shapes and textured layers, silhouettes and typography. She's worked with a broad range of publishing clients as well as packaging and in-store work for high street giants and murals on Carnaby Street.

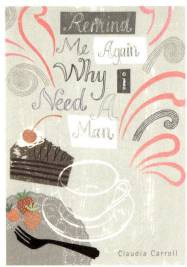

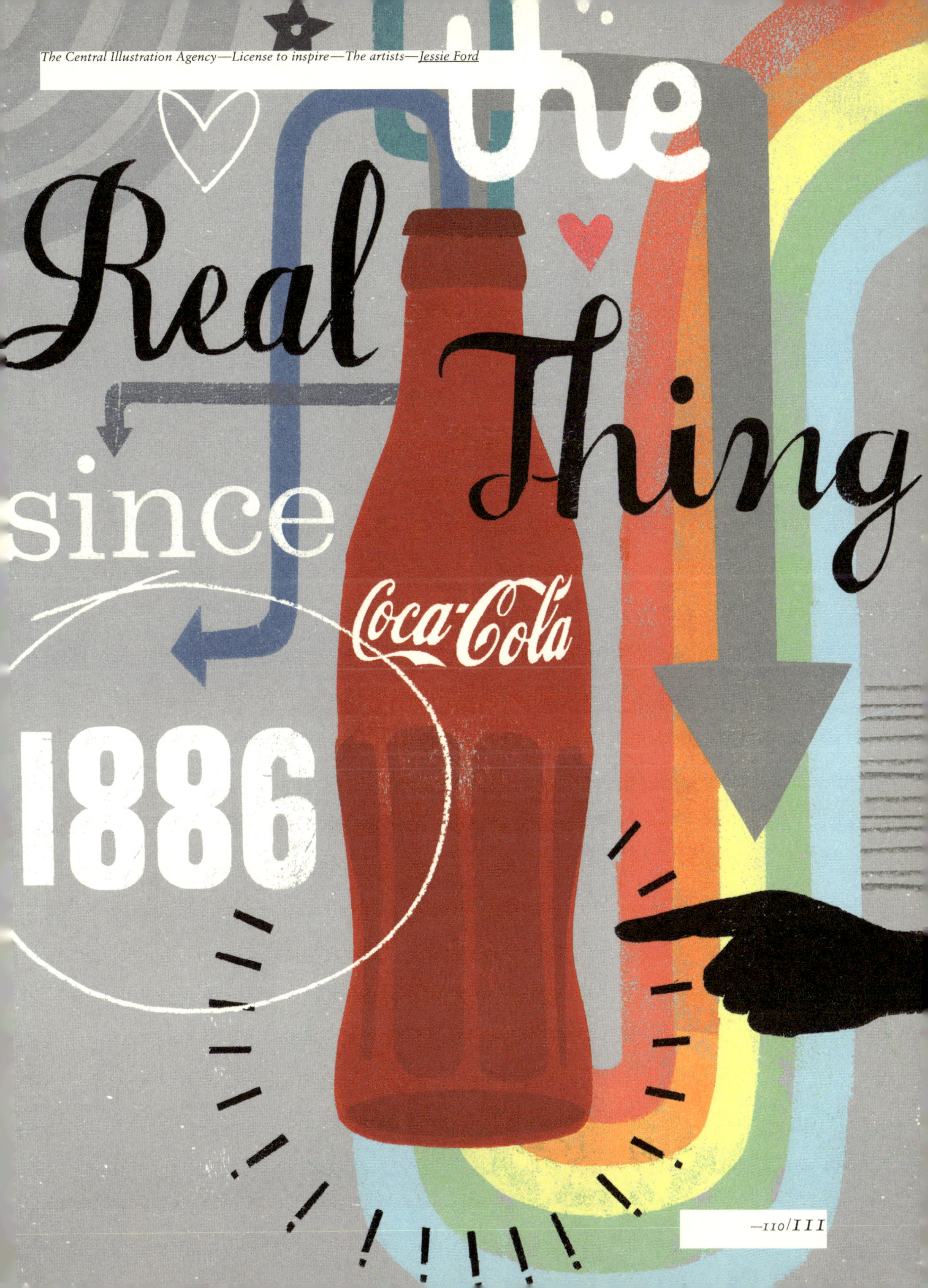
the
Real
Thing
since
1886
Coca-Cola

—Andrew Foster

*Andrew practices both fine art and commercial art. Everyday meaning forms
the crux to his ideas, marks and communication. Regularly breaking out of the
conventional physical confines of printed page or poster, he has produced
installation work for London Fashion Week, Kiehls and famously covered every
window of Liberty, London. Andrew is the Subject Leader on the
Communication Design MA at Central Saint Martins.*

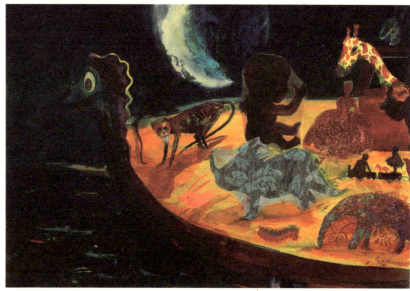

—Nathan Fox

Born in Washington DC in the mid-70s, Nathan suffered an early addiction to cartoons, commercials and video games. This eye-watering fixation combined with an art school training in Kansas City led to a lifelong exploration of narrative art and the over-stimulation associated with his generation. His work has appeared, frankly, everywhere.

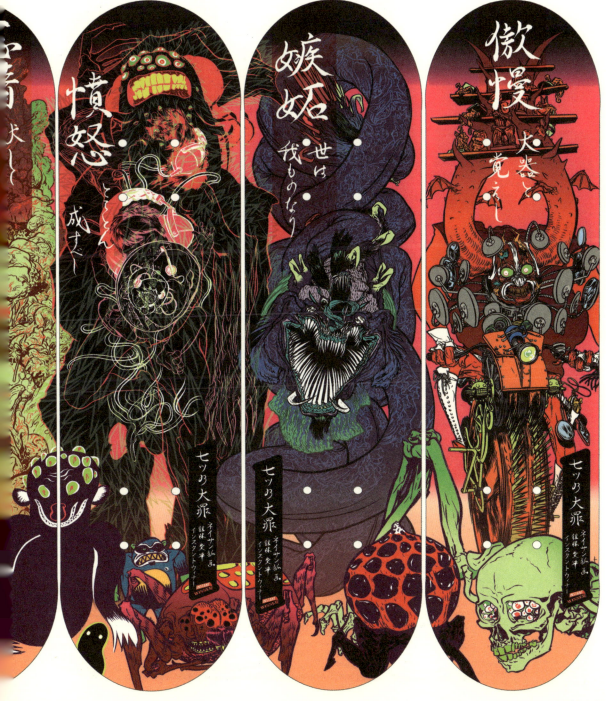

—Jonathan Gibbs

Educated at the Central School of Art and the Slade, Jonathan works in wood engraving, drawing and painting. Living in Scotland he regularly exhibits in Edinburgh and London and is Head of Illustration at Edinburgh College of Art. His visual language is fastidious, linear and deeply sensitive to place.

—Chris Gilvan Cartwright

A Royal Overseas League Travel Bursary to India and Nepal inspired Gilvan Cartwright's luscious and excessive artwork. A Central Saint Martins education and prolific output has helped fill the galleries and private collections of the UK, USA and Japan with his paintings, his commercial clients include the BBC Proms.

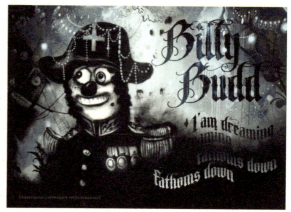

—Good Wives & Warriors

Becky Bolton and Louise Chappell formed this creative partnership having studied together at Glasgow School of Art. Their experimental collaborative approach to illustration and installation has led to exhibitions on just about every continent and projects with Adidas, MTV and Comme des Garçons.

—Brian Grimwood

Renowned illustrator and founder of CIA, Brian has worked extensively across all platforms of commercial art for more years than is polite to mention. Credited by Print magazine as having changed the look of British illustration, Brian's loose, expressive visual language is strongly ideas-led and immediately recognisable.

PITTSBURGH **OPERA**

FALSTAFF

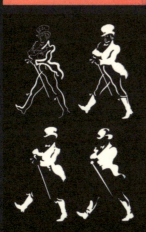

—Martin Haake

He's lived in London, he has a healthy admiration for American folk art, and now he's based in Berlin. Martin is as international as his clients and as well as having a healthy folio of commercial work with Orange, Bacardi and Penguin to name a few, has been extensively published in design annuals and won many awards.

—Pete Harrison

UK designer Pete Harrison has one foot in the commercial art world working with a variety of corporate clients, and the other in the fashion industry running two clothing companies. We don't know where he gets his energy from!

—Lee Hasler

Having finally escaped the lead-filled smog of London to breathe the dung-filled air of the countryside, Lee draws little square-headed folk with one hand and tickles his cat Alfred with the other. When he isn't illustrating for the likes of TBWA, Time Out *and Enterprise IG, he says he parades his tractor around town. We don't believe him, but it's a nice thought.*

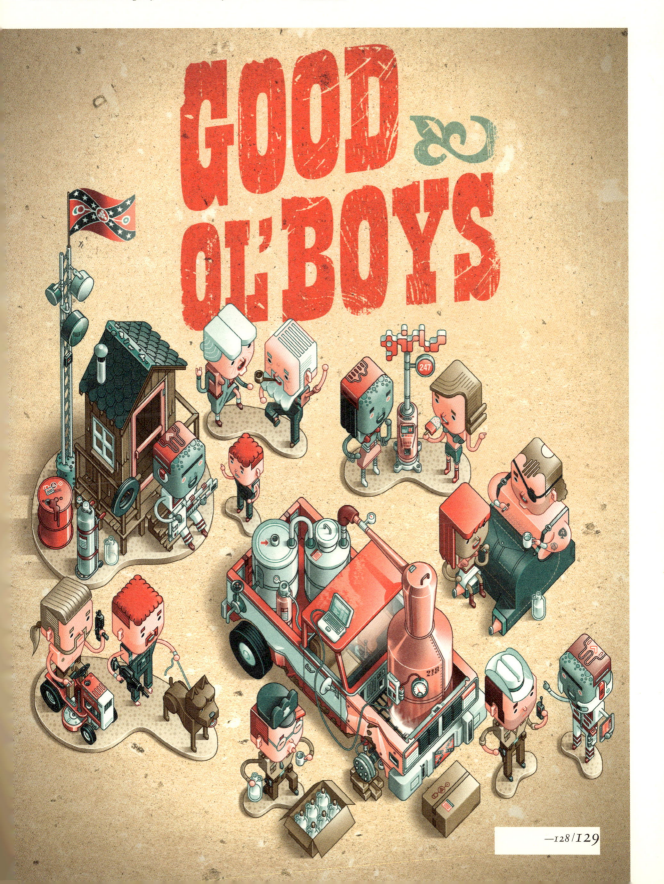

—Sara Hayward

Having lived and worked as a designer and image maker in London, Sara has gravitated back to her rural roots in Devon where she creates illustration for the great and good of the advertising and editorial communities on both sides of the Atlantic.

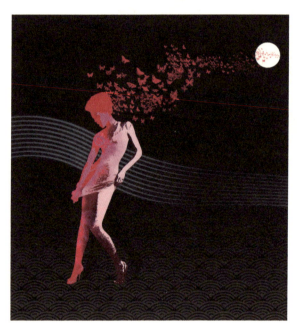

—David Holmes

The achingly dapper David Holmes was born in Chelsea and studied at Ealing College of Art and Central Saint Martins. He began his career in advertising and became the co-founder and Creative Director of Holmes Knight Ritchie. Now based in Primrose Hill he paints, illustrates and travels, all of them beautifully.

—Darren Hopes

Locked in a self-imposed exile from the outside world, Darren lurks in his attic studio hermitage in deepest Cornwall creating visual bait so that the commissioners of the world might be tempted into contacting him. It's worked too! A degree in Photography and a love of paint and found things lead his richly textural illustration.

—Peter Horridge

A founder member of CIA, Peter is one of the world's leading practitioners of calligraphy and typography. His fluidity of line also lends itself to purely illustrative applications, but he is unsurpassed in letterform, his crests, logos and marques have become the identifiers for brands and institutions from Raffles in Singapore to the Scottish Parliament.

—David Hughes

David studied at Twickenham College of Technology, before becoming a freelance illustrator at the age of twenty – in between dabbling with the postal service, TV graphics, and road sweeping. Along came a job from the Observer *and so started a life of commissioned illustration and authorial work which today is best exemplified by his own darkly wonderful book,* Walking the Dog.

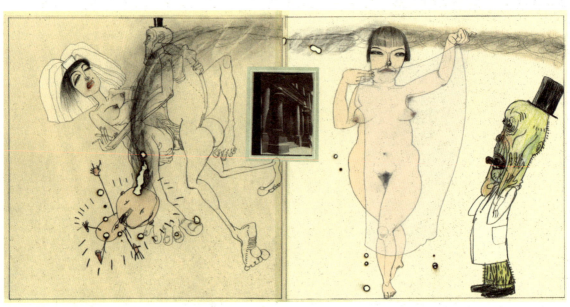

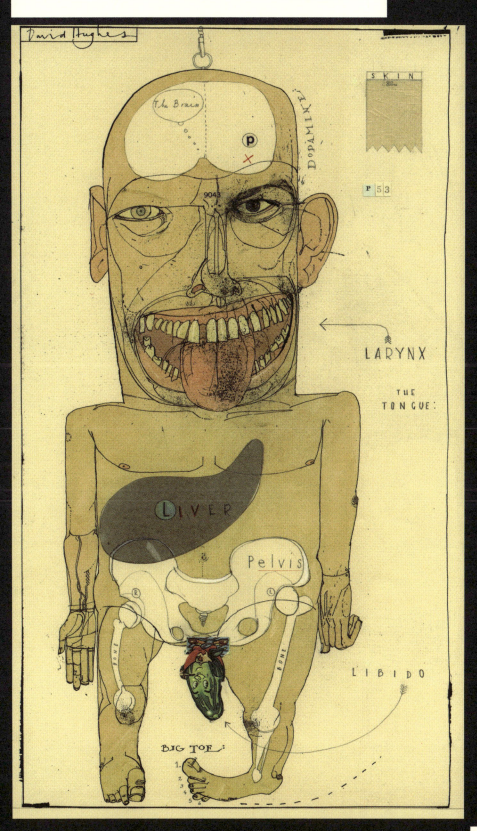

—M.H. Jeeves

M.H. originally studied architecture at Cambridge University before deciding not to inflict her notions of the built environment on the world. Fortunately for us and after some more studying at Central Saint Martins she has since pursued a career in illustration and cartooning for clients ranging from Saatchi & Saatchi to Punch.

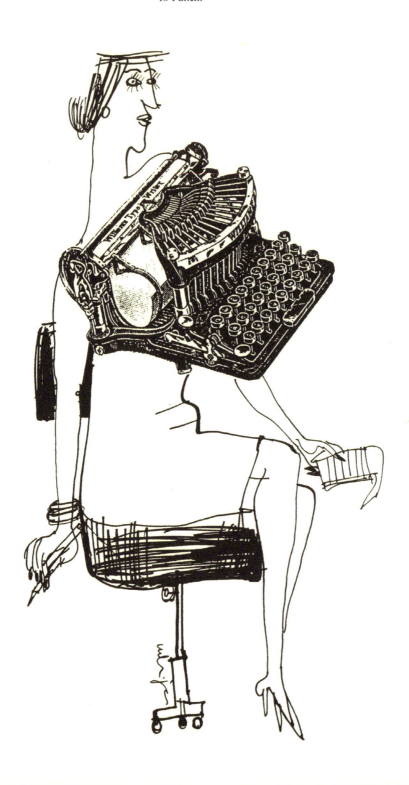

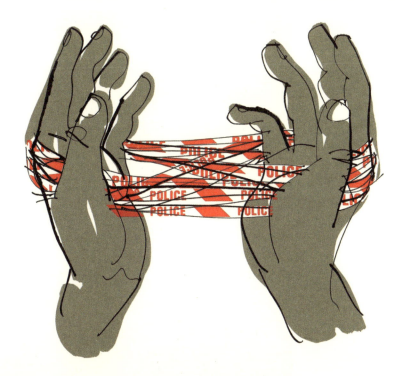

—Kai & Sunny

A prolific, multidisciplinary duo whose work spans the increasingly unstable boundaries between fashion, advertising, design and exhibition. Their intricate, natural and sometimes sinister style has earned them commissions for megabrands like Apple, Becks and Ford as well as countless iconic book covers. Together they are award winners and founders of fashion label Call of the Wild.

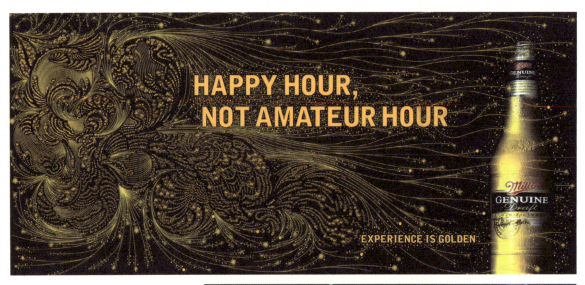

—Chris Kasch

One of our Kingston graduates, Chris Kasch's work draws stylistic parallels with 60s and 70s popular culture but with a highly contemporary edge that separates it from the retro. His highly detailed, instantly recognisable aesthetic has been used by Sony Music, Rolling Stone *and* Vogue.

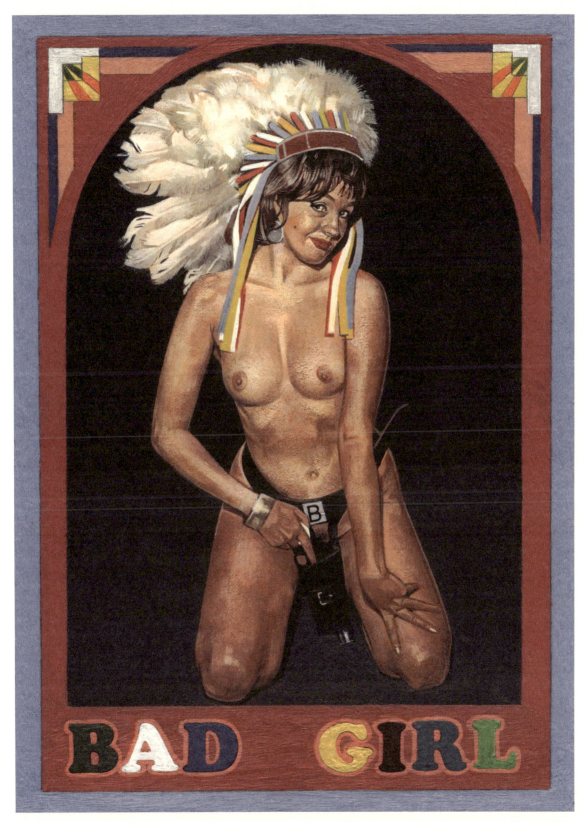

—Carol Lawson

Carol writes and illustrates her own books and her sumptuous painting style graces international advertising and packaging projects. Based on the south coast of England, Carol has illustrated magical texts such as the fairy tales of the Brothers Grimm and Hans Christian Andersen.

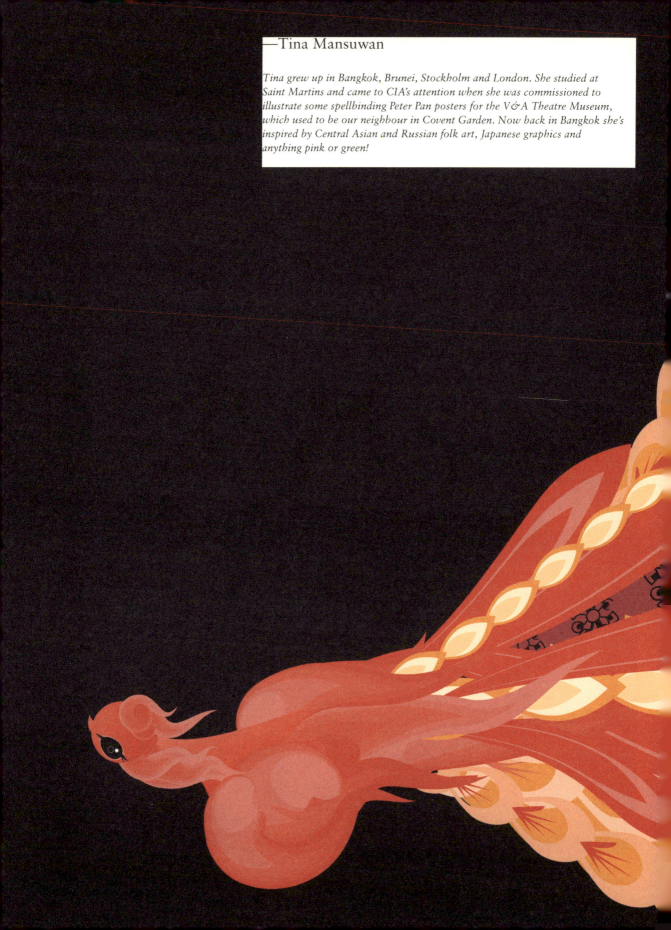

—Tina Mansuwan

Tina grew up in Bangkok, Brunei, Stockholm and London. She studied at Saint Martins and came to CIA's attention when she was commissioned to illustrate some spellbinding Peter Pan posters for the V&A Theatre Museum, which used to be our neighbour in Covent Garden. Now back in Bangkok she's inspired by Central Asian and Russian folk art, Japanese graphics and anything pink or green!

—Tim Marrs

One of our Central Saint Martins' graduates, Tim's work is a frenzied mix of drawing, photography, print and digital techniques and draws on American pulp and pop cultures. His adaptable style has attracted commissions from Nike, Ogilvy and Geffen Records. He lives overlooking the sea on England's south coast.

—Mick Marston

Yorkshire born, Mick exhausted his early ambitions of Premiership football and rock stardom and graduated from Leeds Metropolitan a fully fledged designer. Moving straight into commercial illustration the commissioning world embraced him with high profile jobs and exhibitions both sides of the pond.

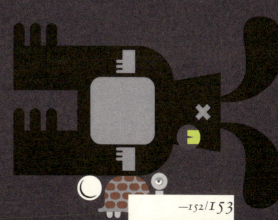

MEGAMUNDEN combines creatures, tattoo design, 80s skate graphics and an essence of the Far East to create his beautiful concoctions. As comfortable painting large scale murals as he is illustrating for advertising or publishing it has been hard to escape MEGAMUNDEN's drawings over recent years. British Airways, Havaianas, Nike, Toshiba, Vodafone, Penguin & The New Scientist are a few amongst many that have fallen for his distinctive creations.

—Chris McEwan

Another of our founder members, Chris is based in Sussex and has established a rich body of surreally graphic illustration for an international roster of clients in publishing, animation and advertising. He regularly exhibits in Paris, Hamburg and London.

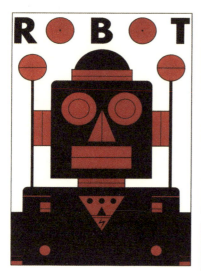

—Clare Melinsky

Clare has lived in Dumfries and Galloway for 30 years where, at the first hint of sunshine, she abandons her 150-year-old printing press for the garden to mulch, snip and hoe, or contemplate the strawberry bed. But when the sun's gone in she lino-cuts for commissions from Royal Mail postage stamps to 80 metre murals and has re-covered the entire works of Shakespeare for Penguin.

—Kate Miller

Kate's illustration originates from a screen-printing background and although now working digitally the processes of layering sketches, photographs and found objects remain constant. Kate is based in Edinburgh and her work has been used widely throughout the design, editorial and advertising sectors.

—Dave Needham

*Dave is based in London but has lived all over the world, which is evident
in his diversely informed artwork. Rumour has it he started drawing aged
two, his talent being spotted when he rendered a pig in chalk on the doorstep.
From there he graduated to working in animation for the likes of Disney and
Cartoon Network and is one of our finest character illustrators.*

High St. France

—Gary Neill

A great example of how to deliver a message in a direct, economical fashion, Gary creates strong simple ideas which cut straight through self indulgence and window dressing. His potent visual style is vibrant and clean and has been used extensively in the fast-paced world of editorial as well as in advertising campaigns.

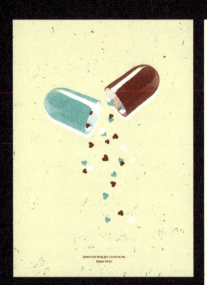

Study nature, love nature, stay close to nature.
It will never fail you.
Frank Lloyd Wright

—Jeff Nishinaka

Born in Los Angeles, paper sculptor Jeff Nishinaka has gained international recognition in the past 15 years through his unique representational 3-dimensional art forms. He has been commissioned to create sculptures for private collectors, publishers, and multi-media clients. Jeff received an honor in 1992 from the Dimensional Illustrators Awards Show in New York and has exhibited in the USA and Japan.

—Paul Oakley

Paul's work sits elegantly within the visual realms of fashion and urban lifestyle. The graphic simplicity of his line work and powerful use of colour has kept Paul in regular demand with publishing, advertising and music clients in London and New York.

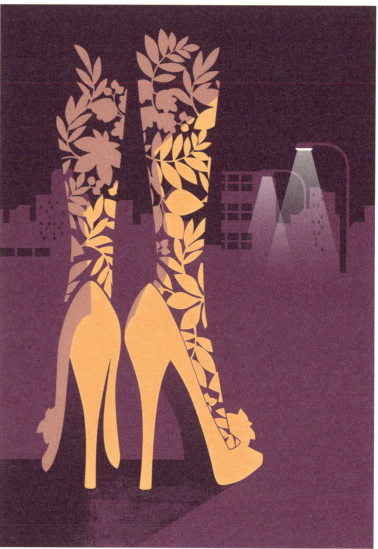

—Nigel Owen

One of our many Central Saint Martins' graduates, Nigel has been illustrating for over 15 years, originally using the traditional crafts of painting and print making before moving his operation onto the computer and reassembling his textural aesthetic onscreen. Nigel is also a senior lecturer on the fantastic Illustration BA course at Falmouth.

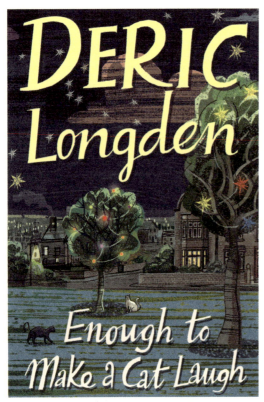

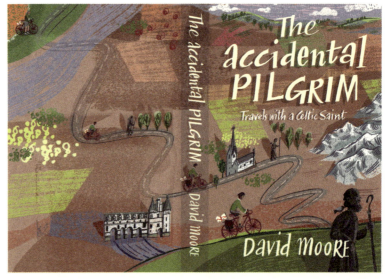

—Jackie Parsons

Surrounded by her vast collection of found paper and printed ephemera, Jackie creates handmade graphic imagery combining collage, print and photography. Living and working on the south coast of England, Jackie has been commissioned worldwide for packaging, book covers and brand development and has won critical acclaim in the Best of British Illustration *annuals.*

—Jitesh Patel

*Being an Indian born in England, Jitesh has two cultures to inspire him.
The Indian brings out the vibrancy in his richly coloured and patterned work,
whereas the British side of him is more considered. He doesn't go a day without
working and his sketchbooks go wherever he does. Jitesh's clients include British
Airways, John Lewis and HSBC.*

—Pirates

A collaborative group set up by Jimi Crayon, Pirates are there for when a conventionally printed execution just won't do. Huge scale installations and murals, permanent or temporary, interior or exterior are what they do best and with a team of artists from a diverse range of backgrounds, they're visually incredibly versatile.

—Wendy Plovmand

Wendy was born and studied in Denmark, graduating with an MA from its Design School in 2001. From there she co-founded the Danish design studio Underwerket and has studied further in London, Paris and New York. Her clients include Selfridges, Philip van Heusen and the Guardian and she regularly exhibits in London and Europe.

—Ulla Puggaard

Ulla began studying just before computer technology became the dominant tool in design education and therefore adopted the root principles of typography and illustration with pen and ink. Image making is her chosen mode of communication and she thrives on the interaction involved in visual problem solving.

—Maria Raymondsdotter

Maria is a Stockholm-based illustrator working with a wide range of international clients. Her work can be seen in magazines from Japan to Paris, advertising campaigns in London, on packaging in Scandinavia, shop interiors in Stockholm and printed wall designs in a coffee shop on the west coast of Sweden.

—John Royle

When it comes to raw punch and dynamism, the blatant foreshortened drama of comic book illustration is about as energetically graphic as it gets. And if CIA are going to represent a comic illustrator, it might as well be a genuine Marvel Comics illustrator. His name's John Royle and he's the real thing!

—Harriet Russell

Harriet studied at Glasgow followed by Saint Martins and she really hasn't stopped drawing since. As well as a multitude of commercial clients including The New York Times *and Channel 4, Harriet is the author/illustrator of several art books including her famous* Envelopes *book and regularly exhibits in London and New York.*

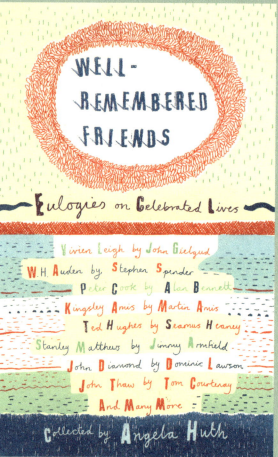

P. G. Wodehouse

A good egg

Jeeves and the Impending Doom

—Jeremy Sancha

After learning his craft at Central Saint Martins and Winchester, Jeremy bought at auction an Albion Press for linocut print-making and set up a studio in London. He has worked with most of the British broadsheets as well as producing wonderfully designed packaging for the likes of Crabtree & Evelyn, Waitrose and ad work for American Express.

THE CIVIL WAR 1642-51
fought between the forces of KING
& PARLIAMENT: *Pikeman* ♣♣♣♣♣

THE CIVIL WAR 1642-51
fought between the forces of KING
& PARLIAMENT: *Drummer* ♣♣♣

THE CIVIL WAR 1642-51
fought between the forces of KING
& PARLIAMENT: *Musketeer* ♣♣♣

THE CIVIL WAR 1642-51
fought between the forces of KING
& PARLIAMENT: *Standard Bearer*

—Yuko Shimizu

Yuko grew up mostly in Tokyo and earned a degree from Waseda University in Marketing and Advertising. She worked for some time in PR before moving to New York to study illustration and pursue her childhood dream. She has worked for everyone from MTV to Playboy and won Art Directors Club awards and a D&AD pencil along the way.

—Paul Slater

After graduating from the RCA, Paul's work quickly became a staple of British newspapers and magazines before breaking into the broader spheres of advertising with clients such as Volkswagen, British Airways and Shell. His uniquely eccentric view of British quirkiness is unrivaled in its wit and weirdness, leading the Independent on Sunday *to list him among the UK's 10 leading illustrators.*

POPULAR SUMMER VISITORS

a. The Lapfowler.
b. The Black-Hearted Ouzal.
c. The Noisy Badstart.
d. The Kirby Whiffler.
e. The Common Ostrich.
f. The Wall Orphan.
g. The Hedge Turkey.
h. The Pocket Dipper.
i. The Humber Hawk.
j. The Masked Smew.
k. The Rented Suit.
l. The Brown Heron.
m. Private Edgar Plover.

THE TREACLE CLASS SUBMARINE
POPULARLY KNOWN AS 'H.M.S. CAREFREE.'

KEY TO EXTERIOR WORKING OF CRAFT
(1) Front end. (2) Hatch handle. (3) Reinforced glass port hole. (4) Fresh air intake and flap valve. (5) Hatch hinge. (6) Cargo hatch and release port. (7) Cork bung. (8) Very expensive 'Treacle Class' propeller. (9) U-pin. (10) Bottom.

KEY TO INTERIOR WORKING OF CRAFT
(a) Footall bore profile. (b) Navigation rod. (c) Helmsman. (d) Hand pumped air compressor. (e) Cargo hold piston mechanism. (f) Cargo hold and cargo. (g) Knowsley and Strident,' marine inboard motor.

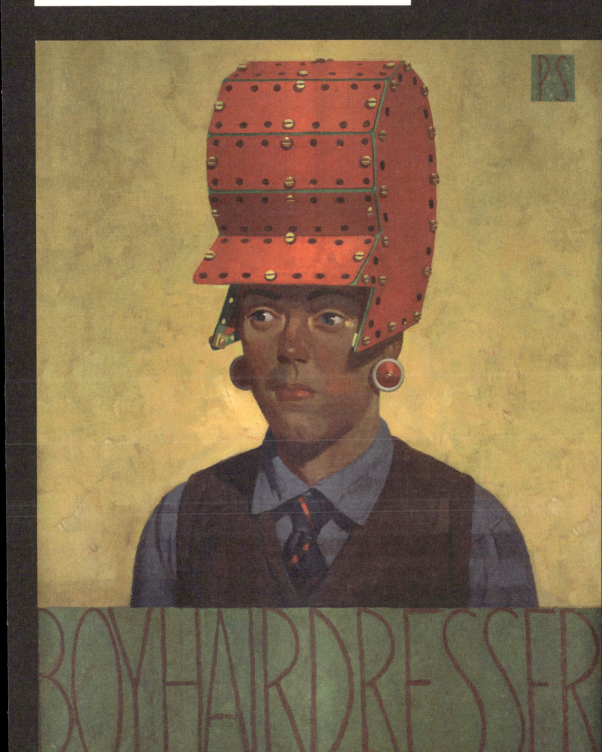

—Ray Smith

Despite the grey of Ray's home city of London, his illustration is a joyous exploration of intricate pattern and flamboyant colour. His output mixes commissioned work for the likes of Absolut and Nike with personal illustration and animation projects, which he exhibits in the UK and USA.

—John Spencer

An art school education was only the start of an ongoing passion for learning about print. Stints living and working throughout Europe were interspersed by learning wood engraving, then stone lithography, then letterpress, skills that John puts to exceptionally good use in the appreciative worlds of publishing and advertising.

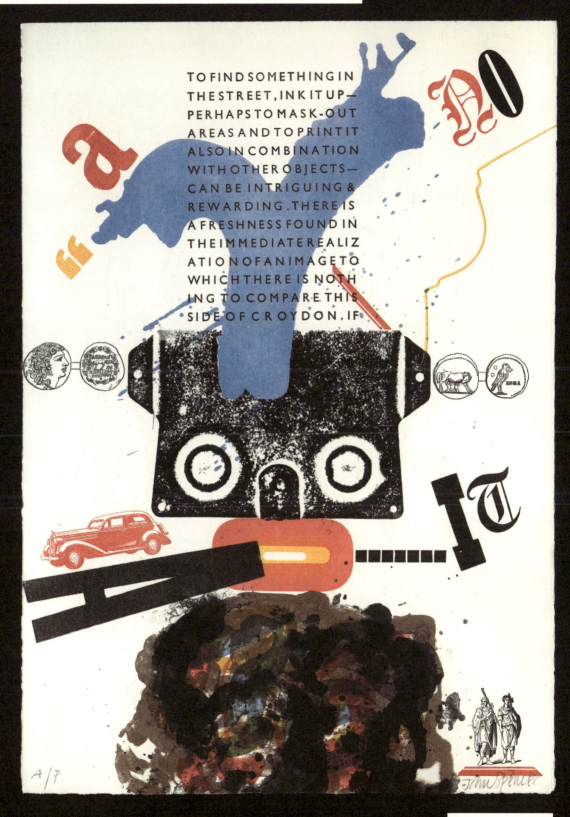

TO FIND SOMETHING IN
THE STREET, INK IT UP—
PERHAPS TO MASK-OUT
AREAS AND TO PRINT IT
ALSO IN COMBINATION
WITH OTHER OBJECTS—
CAN BE INTRIGUING &
REWARDING. THERE IS
A FRESHNESS FOUND IN
THE IMMEDIATE REALIZ
ATION OF AN IMAGE TO
WHICH THERE IS NOTH
ING TO COMPARE THIS
SIDE OF CROYDON. IF

A/P

—Simon Spilsbury

Simon is primarily an exponent of line, the quality of which his commissioners have described as spontaneous, energetic, quirky, inherently humorous, adaptable and elegant. One enthusiastic New York Art Director said 'Spilsbury's drawings always jump off the page and bite me on the ass.' Quite good if you're trying to reach an audience!

—Spiral Studio

Spiral Studio is Darren Hopes' alter ego, giving him the opportunity to indulge his more photographic leanings. His esoteric erotica has gained critical acclaim in fine art circles but also found its way into the commercial sector among publishing clients and ad work for clients such as Pretty Polly.

—Louisa St. Pierre

The boundlessly energetic Louisa ran CIA for several years before heading to the States where she runs the Illustration and Interactive divisions of Bernstein and Andriulli as well as being the Managing Editor of Spread magazine. Her illustration work is inspired by Byzantine religious art, folk art and Klimt.

—Mark Thomas

Having grown up on a diet of American Pulp, Mark studied illustration before embarking on a freelance career in the UK which spread into Europe and the USA. Prolific and adaptable in equal measure he's worked in all areas of illustration including movie posters, ad campaigns and book jackets.

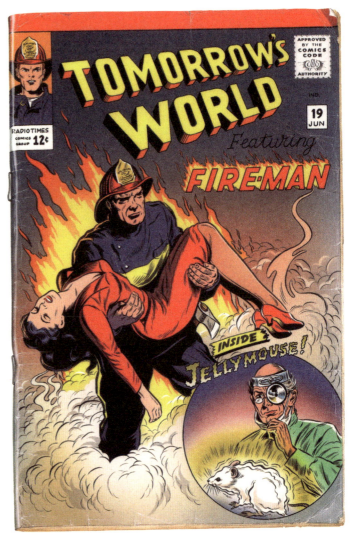

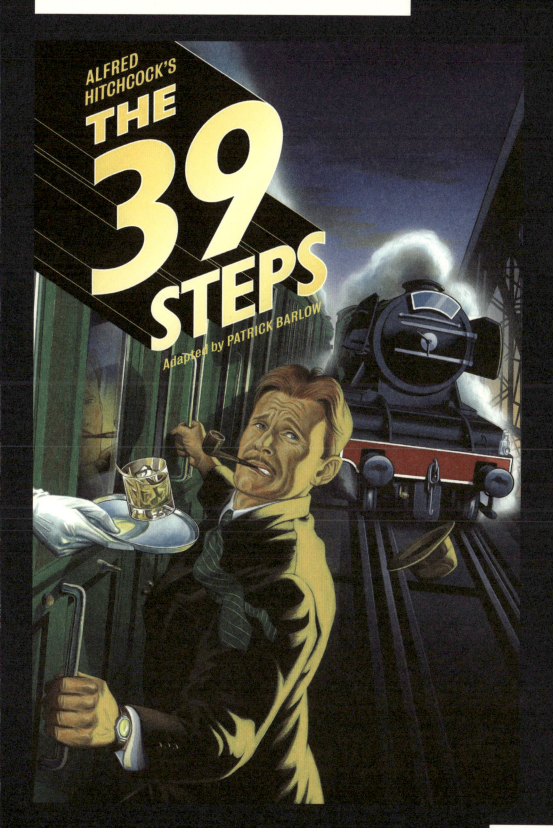

—Alex Turvey

Alex is a director, designer and illustrator with an eclectic oeuvre of projects ranging from music videos, fashion, films and commercials. Having grown up by the sea in Cornwall, he now lives by the river in London and sums up his personal visual indulgences as textural landscapes, anatomical drawings and glitter. Well, Shakira, Nike, MTV and Budweiser seem to share his eccentric tastes!

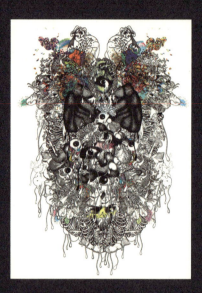

—Benjamin Wachenje

Benjamin started out as a spray can artist before studying at Camberwell. His illustrations continue to be influenced by the early hip-hop movement and contemporary street culture. A regular contributor to the Guardian *and* Rolling Stone, *he has also collaborated with Timberland, Levi's, Virgin Atlantic and Rockstar Games.*

—Paul Wearing

*Paul's an RCA graduate and based in London. A born traveller he has worked
extensively throughout the US and Far East with fashion, interior and advertising
houses. The influence of his design background is evident in much of his
illustration and has led to high profile campaign work as well as huge-scale
architectural installations.*

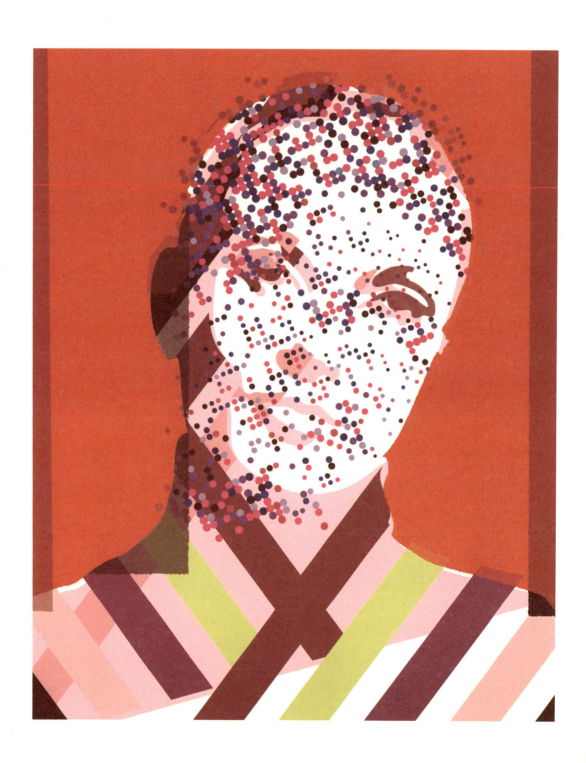

—Richard Wilkinson

After a Fine Art degree and brief career as an electronic musician, Richard worked in London as a sound designer, which led to commercials production and then motion graphics. In 2006 he returned to his visual roots and as an illustrator has worked with the Telegraph, TBWA, Saatchi & Saatchi and Harper Collins.

—Mike Wilks

After art school, Mike set up his own design group, TWD, in 1970. Five years later after great success he sold up and began a new career writing and illustrating his own books. The Ultimate Alphabet *and* The Ultimate Noah's Ark *were bestsellers and for a while lived in a 13th century stone mas in the South of France where he was the subject of an award-winning documentary on his life and work. Now back in London he continues to produce illustrated books and novels, commercial illustration work and fine art paintings.*

www.
central
illustration
.com

In conversation with <u>Sir Peter Blake</u>
at his studio

'I make a distinction between my
fine art practise and commercial work
through the scheduling of my week.
I come into the studio during the day to
work on commissioned pieces whereas
my evenings are given to personal
projects. Considering that one such
personal undertaking is a drawing
project that has been in progress for ten
years, the comparative immediacy of
commissioned illustration, the necessary
rapidity of ideas is a welcome exercise
which keeps me sharp. What excites me
is the contrast'.

IAN DURY

The Definitive Biography

WILL BIRCH

One such recent commercial project from Pan Macmillan saw Peter producing cover art for the recent biography of Ian Dury, a man Blake knew very well as an artist and musician. Peter taught Dury while he was studying at Walthamstow Art College and again when Dury went on to study painting at the RCA. His work had graphic qualities in common with Peter's and on occasion when Peter received commissions he didn't have time to take on, he would pass the opportunity on to Ian.

Dury didn't pursue a career in painting and turned his attention to music but they remained friends and for one of Blake's shows which featured music playing in each room of the exhibition, Dury wrote the song Peter the Painter. In later years following Blake's move to Somerset, Dury would let him know whenever he was touring in the area and the Blockheads would descend Peter's home, post-gig and *en masse*, in the early hours of the morning.

—4

BACK–WORD WHAT INSPIRES BRIAN GRIMWOOD

Inspiration has surrounded me since when, as a 3-year-old boy I'd play drawing games with my father. I would make an indiscernible scribble and hand it to him, he would turn it into a recognisable picture then we would swap roles and do the same in reverse. This game and its emphasis on quick-fire idea generation has influenced me to this day and my work still retains a gestural spontaneity born of the hand trying to keep up with the eye.

Like many a young commercial artist of that era, my childhood was influenced by comics and Disney but also by sneaky trips to the library to trace Leonardo da Vinci

—*Brian and his father with whom he would play*
drawing games, plus an early school photograph

drawings onto toilet paper. Whenever the school play was on, I was the first to volunteer for scene painting and can still keenly remember the sweet smell of kindergarten powder paint.

A great inspiration to me in my formative years was Owen Frampton who ran the three year art course at Bromley Tech, which I attended from the age of thirteen. He was a great supporter of my ambitions to pursue a career in the graphic arts and remains a figure that I list alongside my parents, The Beatles and Sonny Boy Williamson as some of the principal role models of my teens.

Despite Bromley Tech taking me from the tender age of thirteen to sixteen, those

—Brian, second row from the top at Bromley Tech. And just a few places to the left, a young David Bowie

three years were my equivalent of a degree complete with the long hair, all-night Blue-Nun-fuelled parties and the encouragement to express myself through my own visual language. The music, art and mentoring of the day gave me the confidence to simply be myself and communicate in an honest and fluent manner, and there were many sources of inspiration during those formative years.

Fellow pupils included David Jones, later to become David Bowie, an individual who I would go on to bump into numerous times in coming years and ultimately support with my own band when Bowie was playing the Marquee club in Soho. David's relentlessness in pursuing his dream was infectious and a tangible example of how

—*After returning from World War II, Owen Frampton taught Life Drawing at Beckenham School of Art. He was then asked to head the Art Department at a new school, Bromley Technical High School for Boys.*

His inspirational course introduced & nurtured Art & Design to many now, well known Artists, Designers & Musicians, many of whom would otherwise, not have had the chance of such an education. Photo courtesy of Clive Frampton.

given the talent and enough ambition, anything really was possible.

Another classmate was Chris Dyer who invited me to accompany him to his sister's ballet class to draw the dancers. Watching him work completely changed the way I approached drawing. Whereas before I would struggle to achieve a likeness of a pose, Chris would somehow see his subject as a whole picture. I learned a great deal from this experience which built on the infant scribbling games played with my father in encouraging me to see the idea in its entirety even before ink touched paper.

On leaving Bromley, Owen Frampton got me my first job at a major London studio called Carlton Artists where I worked alongside calligraphers and typesetters, printmakers and fashion illustrators. This proved to be an invaluable experience which led to an art director position at Pye Records in 1965, a very exciting time to be designing record sleeves and working alongside many of the musicians who'd influenced me throughout my teens.

Some of my illustrative output during this time was quite formally rendered, not laboured as such but certainly carefully considered. I recognised that stylistically it was my initial doodles that were unique to me, they had a special quality, a gestural freedom that was true to the idea.

I got myself a studio in Covent Garden and in the following years gently moved away from conventional employment and established myself as an illustrator.
Today I'm still based in my studio, actively

working as a commercial artist but the
studio has now moved to the green hills of
the English south coast. Now as always, it's
harder to identify what doesn't inspire me
than what does. Many of the artists,
musicians and friends that I've had the
privilege to encounter in my youth remain
with me now and I'm still playing bass
with my band. Many of my
contemporaries draw my admiration,
David Holmes, Jeff Fisher, David Hughes,
Paul Slater, Bush Hollyhead, Chris Corr,
Tony Meeuwissen, Linda Gray and Peter
Till to name a few. Being surrounded by
creativity is infectious and spending time
with other artists challenges me to
continue to evolve as an artist.

You can never stop learning. Every face is
worth drawing, every country visited has
its own cultural influences to bear. Eyes
and mind are always open to that question

that requires a drawn or painted answer. Right now in 2010 I'm continuing to question my working methodology, introducing new catalysts to kick-start the creative process and keep myself excited. Whereas in the past I have had a resolved mental image of how an illustration will look prior to committing it to paper, I'm now relinquishing a certain degree of control and allowing the process to inform and influence the direction of my artwork. I'll lay down certain component elements and let serendipity play a role in how those elements come together.

I feel this has brought a certain maturity to my approach. I haven't lost any of the spontaneity that my work has always had, but this new process of conversational reassessment means that I'm creating an element of surprise which is tremendously exciting for me.

In conversation with <u>Katie Grogan,</u>
freelance artbuyer

'I always view the whole process as a collaborative exercise. I'm as responsible as the artist for making the commissioned piece work so in a sense it's all in the brief. If the brief is strong enough then belief in the artist will carry you through. It's about allowing the artist the freedom to interpret the concept, to allow them to do what they do best and contribute in such a way that is truly inspirational, enhancing the idea presented in the initial concept. Trust plays a huge part, established relationships can make an enormous difference, if not with the artist then their agent, which in my line of work is often the case. You do need to be able to recognise if it's not quite going where you need it to so being brave, diplomatic and speaking up on both sides plays an important part.

It's become a way of life looking at books, magazines, film, music, blogs, going to exhibitions, degree shows and travel. I find inspiration in it all, you can never see or do too much. I feel sad for those who look no further than their computer, they miss out.'

Index of artists

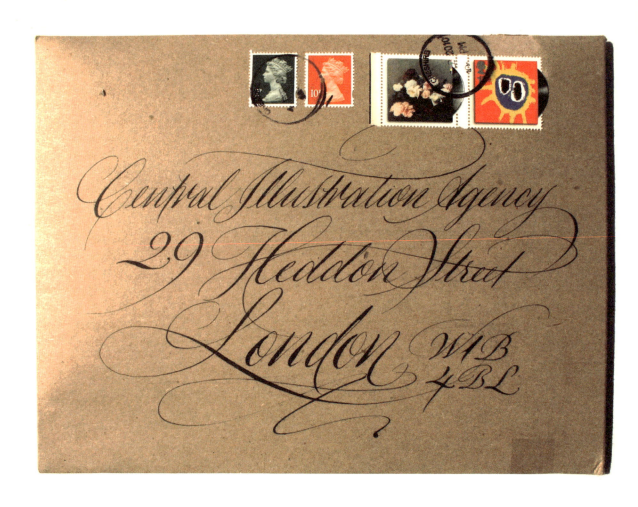

*If you'd like to know more about
the agency or discuss a project with
one of our artists, we'd love to hear
from you...*

Central Illustration Agency
29 Heddon Street, Mayfair, London W1B 4BL

+44(0)20 7734 7187
info@centralillustration.com

www.centralillustration.com